the
CARIBBEAN
pantry cookbook

Steven Raichlen

Photographs by Martin Jacobs

the CARIBBEAN
pantry cookbook

CONDIMENTS AND SEASONINGS FROM
THE LAND OF SPICE AND SUN

ARTISAN *New York*

Editor: Ann ffolliott
Production director: Hope Koturo

Published in 1995 by Artisan,
a division of Workman Publishing Company, Inc.
708 Broadway
New York, NY 10003-9555

Library of Congress Cataloging-in-Publication Data
Raichlen, Steven.
The Caribbean pantry cookbook : condiments and seasonings from the land of spice and sun / Steven Raichlen ;
photographs by Martin Jacobs.
    Includes bibliographical references and index.
    ISBN 1-885183-10-0 (alk. paper)
    1. Condiments—Caribbean Area.
2. Spices—Caribbean Area.
3. Cookery, Caribbean. 1. Title.
TX819.A1R34   1995
641.6'521'09729—dc20   95-17489

Printed in Italy
10 9 8 7 6 5 4 3 2 1
First Printing

To Barbie on the beach

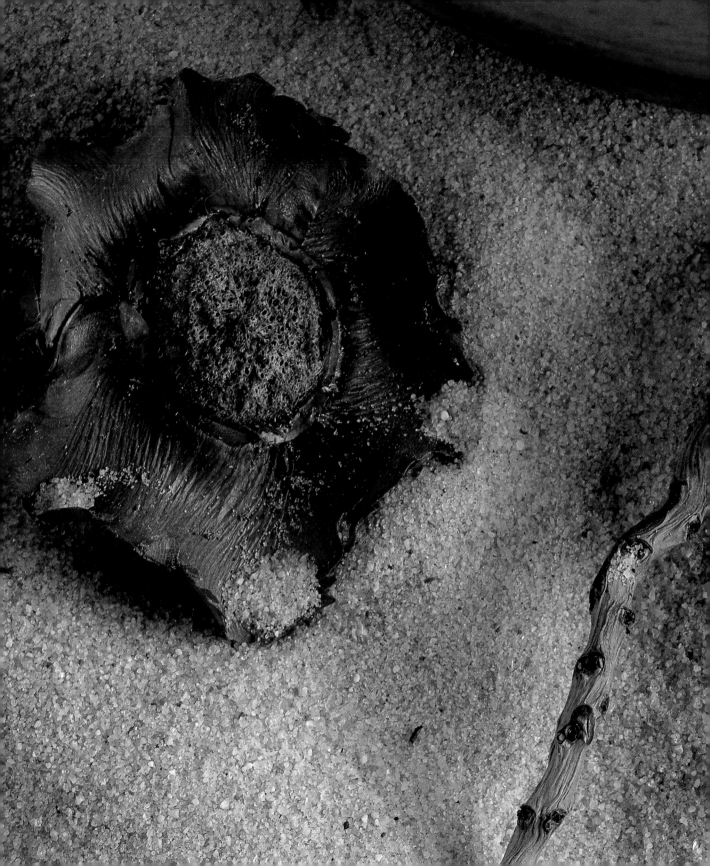

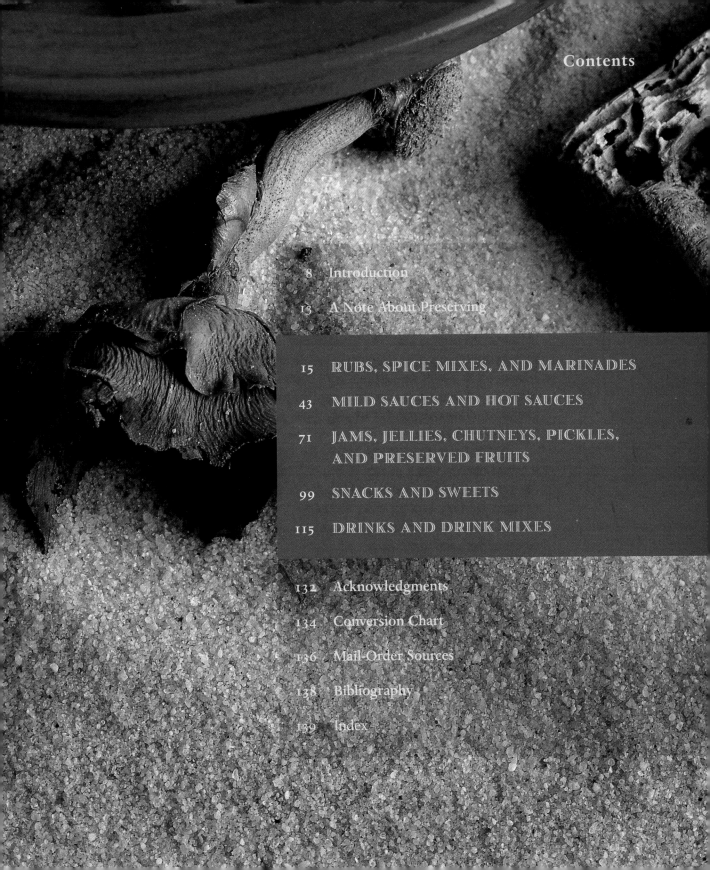

Contents

Introduction

CARIBBEAN. The very word evokes vibrant images of flavor sensations and tropical abundance. The Caribbean is a realm of gustatory extremes: soothing rum drinks and mouth-searing hot sauces; fiery spice rubs and fragrant marinades; pungent preserves and dulcet jams. Caribbean cooking is laid-back and low-key, offering bold flavors that match the intensity of the tropical sun.

This is certainly true of the jams, jellies, spice rubs, table sauces, spiced rums, and sweets that constitute the Caribbean pantry. There are few places in the world where you find such a diverse assortment of seasonings and condiments. Spicy snacks to nibble while watching a Caribbean sunset. Tangy table sauces to awaken heat-wilted appetites. Festive rum drinks to sip while swaying to the rhythmic pulse of steel drums.

Necessity was the mother of invention for many Caribbean condiments. Food spoils quickly in the tropical heat. The islanders had no choice but to develop elaborate techniques for salting, pickling, curing, smoking, and candying to preserve foods without refrigeration. Jamaica's jerk—pork steeped in a fiery paste of chilies and spices and smoke-grilled over allspice wood fires—was a way to extend the meat's shelf life. A venerable tradition of candy and jam making ensured that tropical fruits picked at peak ripeness could be enjoyed for many months to come.

The richness of the Caribbean pantry has been shaped by the region's unique agriculture and climate. Visit a market in Pointe-à-Pitre or Port of Spain and you'll be dazzled by the profusion of tropical vegetables, exotic fruits, and intensely flavored whole spices. Grenada certainly lives up to its nickname "Spice Island," supplying most of the world's nutmeg. Cacao and vanilla beans grow wild in Guadaloupe's tropical forests, while chives, culentro, mint, and thyme carpet Trinidad's Paramin Hills. It's not just an accident of history that herbs and spices figure so prominently in Caribbean cooking. The West Indies are where these ingredients grow.

But the driving force of the region's food is its incredible ethnic diversity. Caribbean cooking is a patchwork quilt of colors, textures, and flavors—a multiethnic tapestry woven from the cuisines of Europe, Africa, the New World, and even Asia. Many islands changed hands dozens of times, with each new conqueror adding flavors to the local melting pot. The diversity of races and languages in the region is reflected in the Caribbean pantry.

Condiments and seasonings have long played a prominent role in Caribbean cooking. The first settlers were the Arawak Indians, a peaceful race of fishermen and farmers who cultivated such New World foods as sweet potatoes, corn, and cassava. The Arawaks seasoned their food with fiery chilies, cassareep (cassava root vinegar), and annatto seed, a rust-colored spice with an earthy, almost iodine flavor. Cassareep remains a key ingredient in Bajan pepperpot (a soulful stew made with oxtail, chicken, salt beef, and other meats); annatto seed is used in Cuban *arroz con pollo* (rice with chicken); and Puerto Rican *asopao* (a soupy stew of rice and seafood). As for chilies, the incendiary Scotch bonnet is one of the defining flavors of Caribbean cooking.

The arrival of the Spanish in 1492 introduced a host of new foods to the region, from wine and olive oil to vinegar and European spices. Metal cooking utensils from Spain greatly improved Caribbean kitchen technology, as did durable containers made from metal and glass. An ancient Spanish vinegar-based meat seasoning became Cuba's national marinade, adobo. (It's now made with sour orange juice, cumin, and garlic.)

Columbus brought sugarcane to the Caribbean on his second voyage in 1494. It wasn't long before the Old World technique of distillation created a New World spirit that remains the quintessential drink of the Caribbean: rum. Virtually every nation in the Caribbean produces its own rum, with styles varying widely from island to island. In Guadaloupe and Martinique, for example, rum is made from fresh sugarcane juice, not molasses. Most rum is distilled in industrial continuous stills, but a few brands, like Haiti's Barbancourt, use the traditional pot still of Cognac and Scotland. Jamaican distillers once favored "dunder" rums, made like sour mash whisky in Kentucky. (Dunder is a portion of the fermented molasses— added the way a *levain* is to sourdough bread.) Connoisseurs in the French West Indies prize *rhum vieux*, "old rum," which acquires a brandylike complexity after lengthy aging in oak barrels. Armed with rum and the local tropical fruits, New World bartenders created a cocktail tradition that has inspired mixologists all over the world.

Eager for a share of New World wealth, the French, Dutch, and British colonized the islands in turn. Each nation put its mark on the local larder. In the French islands, for example, one finds French-style jams, rum-preserved fruits, and a tropical vinaigrette called *sauce chien*. The Dutch influence lives on in the *pika* (chili-fired pickled onions). The British heritage is apparent in the fruit cheeses and ginger beer found on most of the English-speaking islands.

The arrival of the first African slaves in the seventeenth century had a profound impact on Caribbean culinary history. Brought here to work the sugar plantations that stretched from Cuba to Trinidad, the slaves introduced such traditional African foods as gunga peas (gandoles), okra, and yams (a true yam is quite different from what we call a sweet potato). Denied fresh meat and fish (deemed too expensive), the slaves evolved a cuisine based on inexpensive ingredients, such as "ground provisions" (starchy root vegetables), beans, salt fish, and salt pork. Many Caribbean hot sauces and condiments were perfected by the Afro-Caribbeans to lend excitement to an otherwise monotone diet.

When slavery was abolished in the nineteenth century, new groups of immigrants were recruited to work the cane fields. Indentured workers from India brought curry powder to Jamaica and Trinidad and the French version—*colombo*—to Guadaloupe and Martinique. Portuguese laborers were the source of Curaçao's famous fruitcake, *bolo pretu* (literally "black cake"), while Indonesians introduced satays (kebabs) with *pindasaus* (spicy peanut sauce). Chinese workers added Asian spices and vegetables, not to mention Asian-style pickles and chili pastes, to the already cosmopolitan Caribbean pot.

The warm climate of the Caribbean supports a bounty of exotic fruits, from the perfumed guava to the tangy passion fruit. Small wonder that tropical fruit jams and jellies, rum punches, fruit cheeses, and fruit curds became popular West Indian sweets. Nor is it any surprise that the world's sugar capital should produce such a rich tradition of candies and sweets, ranging from tamarind balls to chip-chips (coconut candies).

The West Indies are the home of the world's hottest chili, the Scotch bonnet. (The name comes from its crinkled crown, which, with a little imagination, looks like a Scottish turban.) We're talking major firepower here: the Scotch bonnet and its cousins—the Mexican habanero, Jamaican country pepper, the French West Indian *piment*—are fifty times hotter than the jalapeño chili.

There are several reasons for the local popularity of such fiery chilies. The capsaicin in chilies fosters perspiration, the body's natural cooling mechanism. Then there's the "chili high" said to come from eating hot peppers. The body reacts to the painful bite of the hot pepper by producing endorphins, those natural opiates that are responsible for the runner's high. Chilies are also rich in vitamins A and C. It's no accident that some of the world's hottest hot sauces come from the Caribbean islands closest to the equator.

America's love affair with Caribbean flavors began before we were even a country and continues to this day. In the colonial period, rum, molasses, and spices were mainstays of the North American sea trade. During the American Revolution, food, arms, and even Benjamin Franklin's mail were routed through St. Eustatius. Haitian soldiers fought alongside Americans during the War of 1812. The first large-scale arrival of Cuban immigrants in Ybor City and Key West in Florida in the 1860s introduced Caribbean foods and flavors to the North American marketplace. Each new wave of immigrants—Jamaicans to south Florida, Salvadorians to Los Angeles, Puerto Ricans to New York—has increased the availability of West Indian foods.

The reggae revolution of the 1970s furthered North American interest in West Indian cooking. It was only a matter of time before a nation that danced to Bob Marley and Jimmy Cliff discovered the fiery joys of jerk and other Jamaican dishes. The travel boom of the 1980s, with increased air service to the Caribbean, gave many Americans first-hand introductions to the bold flavors of the Caribbean. Having tasted these exciting foods in their countries of origin, we began to crave them at home.

Today North Americans are more interested than ever in the vibrant tastes of the Caribbean pantry. We crave Caribbean seasonings and condiments for many reasons, not least of which is their convenience.

Americans are working harder than ever in these time-starved 1990s. Many of us, much as we love homemade food, simply don't have the time to cook full meals from scratch after work. How nice to be able to enliven a pork chop or fish fillet with a sprinkling of adobo or colombo powder; to jazz up roast chicken with chili lime sauce or green mango chutney; to add interest to frozen yogurt and other desserts with a tropical fruit syrup or rum.

Caribbean condiments are quick and easy to make, and they are convenient to have on hand. Simmer a pound of shrimp in the gutsy Enchilado Sauce on page 66 or the Mamba (spicy Haitian peanut sauce) on page 53, for example, and you've got a great-tasting dinner in minutes.

The bold flavors of the Caribbean pantry have another advantage: health. This fact impressed the first European explorers of the region, who discovered that feeding their crew

West Indian chilies could prevent scurvy during the long sea voyages. Using the intensely flavored marinades and table sauces of the Caribbean, you can turn bland, boring, low-fat foods like pasta and chicken breasts into great-tasting dishes in a matter of minutes. One of the most popular Caribbean cooking techniques is marinating and grilling—the ultimate high-flavor, low-fat cooking method. With all these intense flavorings, Caribbean food doesn't need a lot of added fat to taste rich.

This brings us to the third reason for the exploding interest in Caribbean condiments: their excitement. Culinary historians are quick to point out that in 1991, salsa sales surpassed ketchup in the United States. Spice and chili consumption has skyrocketed in the last decade and is predicted to keep on growing. As a nation we've become impassioned by, even obsessed with, big-flavor foods from the tropics. Few regions can match the gustatory excitement of Caribbean seasonings and condiments.

Finally, in an increasingly automated and anonymous world, most of us cherish an opportunity to make a warm personal gesture. Come holiday time, what better present to offer than something you've made with your own hands? My *Caribbean Pantry* gift list includes boxes of homemade Curry Powder, jars of Orange Pepper Jelly and Banana Jam, and attractive bottles of fruit vinegars and tropical fruits steeped in rum. These gifts will appeal to just about everyone, from the cook, barbecue buff, and chili enthusiast to the armchair traveler or person who left his heart on a beach in Jamaica or St. Barthélemy.

One thing is certain: condiments from *The Caribbean Pantry Cookbook* can make a welcome contribution to your cooking year-round. Born in the tropics and designed to be savored outdoors, Caribbean cooking is ideal for warm-weather entertaining. The emphasis on spices, seasonings, tropical fruits, and fresh vegetables over fat will help keep you looking good in a bathing suit all year. And even in the icy depths of winter, West Indian seasonings can make a great addition to your diet. What better antidote to cold, overcast days and long snowy nights than a blast of spice from the tropics?

I hope you enjoy *The Caribbean Pantry Cookbook*. For me, it's the best way to savor the vibrant flavors of the West Indies without leaving home.

It's hard for many Americans to conceive of a world without refrigeration and failproof food storage. For most of Caribbean history, however, West Indian cooks had to contend with keeping food safe in a hot and steamy climate.

There are numerous ways to stop or slow food spoilage. Techniques include salting, brining, pickling, drying, candying, jam and jelly making, and preserving in alcohol. All have been used with great success by Caribbean cooks over the centuries. Most of these methods are represented in this book.

The most important principle for safe food preservation is cleanliness. Fruits and vegetables should be trimmed of any rotten spots or blemishes. If you use whole fruits, wash them thoroughly before using.

Likewise, your cooking equipment and storage containers should be immaculate. To sterilize bottles or jars, fill them with boiling water and immerse them in a large pot with boiling water to cover by 2 inches. (You may wish to place a rack on the bottom of the pot to keep the jars from rattling.) Boil the jars for 15 minutes. Boil the caps and lids as well. Dip your tongs in the boiling water to sterilize them, too.

Leave the jars in hot water until you're ready to use them.

Remove the jars from the water with tongs and drain well. Add the hot jam, jelly, or chutney to within ⅛ inch of the top of each jar. Place the flat lid on top, rubber side down. Tightly screw on the cap. Invert the filled jar for 10 minutes, then reinvert and let the filling cool. As the filling cools, it will create a vacuum seal.

It's very important to test this seal before putting the jars in your pantry or giving them as gifts. When the jar is properly sealed, the lid will be slightly concave. Press it in the center with your finger—if the lid pops up, the jar isn't properly sealed. Another test is to unscrew the screw band around the jar and lift the jar by the lid. If the lid comes off, the bottle wasn't properly sealed.

Preserves that contain a lot of sugar, salt, vinegar, or natural fruit acids keep the best. Stored in a cool, dark place, they will hold for several months or even up to a year.

RUBS, SPICE MIXES, AND MARINADES

COLOMBO IS THE FRENCH WEST INDIAN version of curry powder. It takes its name from the city of Colombo in Sri Lanka. After the abolition of slavery, the French imported indentured laborers from India and Sri Lanka to work the cane fields in Guadaloupe and Martinique. The Indian influence survives in not only the wide use of colombo powder in Creole cooking but in the humpbacked Brahmin cattle one sees all over Guadaloupe. You can buy commercial colombo powder on the French islands and in West Indian markets in this country. But it's easy to make your own and the results will be far more tasty.

This spice mix contains one offbeat ingredient: roasted rice. Roasting gives the rice a nutty flavor and makes it easier to grind. The rice acts as both a flavoring and a natural thickener.

Colombo Powder makes a great holiday gift from one of the lesser-known cuisines of the Caribbean. Use it in any recipe you would curry powder, especially soups and stews.

OPPOSITE, CLOCKWISE FROM TOP *Garam Masala (page 25), Colombo Powder, fenugreek seeds, black mustard seeds, Puerto Rican Adobo Powder (page 20), whole nutmeg with mace, cardamom pods, Curry Powder (page 21)*

¼ cup white rice

¼ cup cumin seeds

¼ cup coriander seeds

1 tablespoon mustard seeds (preferably black)

1 tablespoon black peppercorns

1 tablespoon fenugreek seeds

1 teaspoon whole cloves

¼ cup turmeric

Cook the rice in a dry skillet over medium heat, shaking the pan frequently, until a light golden brown, about 5 minutes. Transfer the rice to a plate and let cool.

Add the whole spices to the skillet and cook over medium heat, shaking the pan, until lightly toasted and fragrant, about 3 minutes. Transfer the spices to the plate to cool.

Combine the rice and roasted spices in a spice mill or blender and grind to a fine powder. Stir in the turmeric.

Store the powder in a jar or airtight container away from heat and light. It will keep for several months.

Makes 1 cup.

NOTE: Black mustard seeds are hotter than white, but the latter will work in a pinch. Fenugreek seeds are tan and rectangular with a slight but agreeable bitterness. Both are available at East Indian markets, gourmet shops, and natural foods stores.

Lamb Colombo

THE TRADITIONAL MEAT for Colombo in the French West Indies would be kid (*cabri*). But wonderful colombos can be made with lamb, not to mention with beef, pork, chicken, seafood, and vegetables. My version is a little wetter than most; I like to have plenty of gravy to spoon over rice.

A *boniato* is a Caribbean sweet potato, a tapered tuber with purplish skin and a mild white flesh that tastes like roasted chestnuts. It's not as sweet as an American sweet potato. A *calabaza* is a West Indian pumpkin. Both are available at West Indian and Hispanic markets and at an increasing number of supermarkets.

1½ pounds lean lamb (leg or shoulder)

2 tablespoons canola or olive oil

Salt and freshly ground black pepper

1 medium onion, finely chopped

6 garlic cloves, minced

2 bunches of chives or 1 bunch of
   scallions, finely chopped

2 teaspoons minced fresh ginger

3 tablespoons Colombo Powder (page 17), or
   good-quality commercial curry powder

2 teaspoons fresh thyme

5 to 6 cups chicken stock, vegetable stock,
   or water

2 tablespoons tomato paste

1 pound potatoes or *boniatos* (Caribbean
   sweet potatoes), peeled and cut into
   1-inch pieces

1 pound *calabaza* (West Indian pumpkin)
   or butternut squash, peeled, seeded,
   and cut into 1-inch pieces

1 tablespoon fresh lime juice, or to taste

Trim the fat off the lamb and cut the meat into 1-inch cubes. Heat 1 tablespoon oil in a large sauté pan. Season the lamb with salt and pepper and brown it on all sides over high heat, working in several batches to keep from crowding the pan. Transfer the lamb to a platter with a slotted spoon.

Pour off the fat. Heat the remaining 1 tablespoon oil in the pan. Add the onion, garlic, chives, and ginger and cook over medium heat until lightly browned, 4 to 6 minutes. Stir in the Colombo Powder and cook for 1 minute, or until fragrant.

Return the lamb to the pan with the thyme, stock, and tomato paste. Bring the mixture to a boil, reduce the heat, and gently simmer the lamb for 1 hour. Add the potatoes and calabaza and continue cooking for 30 minutes or until the lamb and vegetables are very tender. Add stock or water as necessary to keep the stew moist. The stew can be prepared up to 48 hours ahead to this stage and reheated.

Just before serving, stir in lime juice to taste. Correct the seasoning. Spoon the Colombo over a mound of rice or couscous. Sprinkle the cilantro on top and serve at once.

Serves 6.

Puerto Rican Adobo Powder

ADOBO IS ONE OF THE MOST POPULAR seasonings in the Spanish Caribbean. But what you get when you ask for it varies widely from island to island. In Cuba, *adobo* describes a tangy marinade made with garlic, cumin, and sour orange juice (see page 26). In Mexico, the term refers to a fiery paste of orange juice, garlic, and chipotle (smoked jalapeño) chilies.

In Puerto Rico, adobo is a seasoned salt that is generously sprinkled on meats and seafood prior to grilling, sautéing, or frying. Supermarkets sell commercial blends, which are loaded with monosodium glutamate. Here's a homemade version that lends unexpected excitement to just about any dish.

6 tablespoons kosher salt

2 tablespoons white peppercorns

2 tablespoons cumin seeds

2 tablespoons garlic powder

Combine the salt, peppercorns, and cumin seeds in a dry skillet and cook over medium heat until the spices are lightly toasted and fragrant, about 3 minutes. Transfer the mixture to a bowl to cool.

Combine the roasted spice mixture and garlic powder in a spice mill or blender and grind to a fine powder.

Store the mixture in an airtight container away from heat or light. It will keep for several months.

Makes a little less than 1 cup.

NOTE: Pan-roasting the spices isn't a traditional procedure, but it greatly enhances the flavor.

Curry powder was probably brought to the Caribbean by the British, but the indentured East Indian workers who came to Trinidad in the nineteenth century made it indispensable in West Indian cooking. It enjoys wide popularity on the English-speaking islands, especially Jamaica and Trinidad and Tobago. There's even a French West Indian version called Colombo Powder (see page 17).

Most cooks use a commercial blend, but homemade curry powder will be more flavorful. The secret is to start with whole spices, which contain more aromatic oils than ground ones do. Skillet-roasting the spices imparts a subtle smoky aroma and further intensifies the flavor.

If you're used to commercial curry powder, use this one sparingly to begin with: it will probably be more flavorful than what you're accustomed to.

½ cup coriander seeds

2½ tablespoons black peppercorns

1½ cinnamon sticks (about 4 inches altogether), broken into small pieces

1 tablespoon cardamom pods

1½ teaspoons fenugreek seeds (see Note on page 17)

3 tablespoons turmeric

2½ tablespoons ground ginger

Place the coriander seeds, peppercorns, cinnamon sticks, cardamom, and fenugreek in a dry skillet and cook over medium heat, shaking the pan, until lightly toasted and fragrant, about 3 minutes. Transfer the spices to a bowl to cool.

Place the roasted spices in a spice mill or blender and grind to a fine powder. Add the turmeric and ginger and grind until mixed.

Store the powder in an airtight container away from heat and light. It will keep for several months.

Makes 1½ cups.

Curried Crab and Dumplings

CURRIED CRAB AND DUMPLINGS is one of the national dishes of Trinidad and Tobago, enjoyed with equal gusto among islanders of African, Indian, Chinese, and English descent. The traditional crab would be land crab—a Caribbean crustacean that's tasty but difficult and messy to eat.

In this country, you could use whole blue crab, Dungeness crab, or lump crab meat. For ease in preparation, I call for the latter in this recipe, but instructions on using whole crab can be found in the recipe note. Curried shrimp can be made the same way. (You'd need about 1 pound shrimp.)

1 pound backfin lump crab meat

1 tablespoon butter or oil

1 large onion, finely chopped (about 1½ cups)

2 garlic cloves, minced

2 teaspoons minced fresh ginger

2 to 3 teaspoons Curry Powder (page 21)

½ teaspoon fresh or dried thyme

1½ cups Coconut Milk (page 129)

Salt and freshly ground black pepper

Dumplings (recipe follows)

2 tablespoons finely chopped fresh flat-leaf parsley or cilantro

Pick through the crab meat, removing any pieces of cartilage or shell.

Melt the butter in a large sauté pan. Add the onion, garlic, and ginger and cook over medium-low heat until soft but not brown, 5 to 7 minutes. Add the curry powder and thyme and sauté for 1 minute. Stir in the coconut milk, salt, and pepper and bring to a boil. Reduce the heat and simmer for 3 to 5 minutes, or until well flavored and slightly thickened.

Stir in the crab meat and gently simmer for 5 minutes, adding salt and pepper to taste. Stir in the dumplings and cook until thoroughly heated. Sprinkle with parsley or cilantro and serve at once.

Serves 4.

NOTE: It's virtually impossible to buy land crabs in the United States. If you're using whole crabs, you'll need 4 large blue crabs or 2 Dungeness crabs. If using blue crabs, boil them for 1 minute. Remove the carapace, gills, and entrails and cut the crab bodies in half, leaving the legs attached. Or have your fishmonger do it.

If using Dungeness crabs, which are usually sold cooked, remove the carapace, gills, and entrails, and cut the crab bodies in quarters, again with legs intact.

Dumplings for Curried Crab

CURRIED CRAB IS USUALLY served with dumplings, and Trinidadians take an almost perverse pride in seeing who can make the heaviest ones! Traditionally, the dumplings are rolled into long, thick strips that are said to resemble cows' tongues. The following dumplings are lighter than those I had in Trinidad, but I think you'll find them quite tasty, nonetheless.

1 cup all-purpose flour

½ teaspoon salt

1 teaspoon baking powder

1 tablespoon butter or shortening

⅓ cup milk, or as needed

¼ teaspoon vegetable oil

Sift the flour, salt, and baking powder into a mixing bowl. Cut in the butter or shortening with 2 knives. The mixture should feel coarse and crumbly. Stir in enough milk to obtain a pliable dough. The mixing and kneading can also be done in a food processor fitted with a metal blade.

Knead the dough for a few minutes on a lightly floured work surface. Pinch off 1-inch balls and roll each out with a small rolling pin to form an oval 3 inches long and 1½ to 2 inches wide.

Bring 2 quarts water to a boil with the oil and a little salt. Briskly simmer the dumplings until cooked (they will be firm), 10 to 15 minutes, stirring occasionally. Drain the dumplings in a colander and stir them into the curried crab.

To MOST NORTH AMERICANS, the notion of an East Indian spice mix means curry powder. But in Trinidad and Tobago, another blend enjoys wide popularity: garam masala. If you're used to curry powder, with its pronounced turmeric flavor, this aromatic mixture will taste delectably different.

You can use this Garam Masala in any dish in which you'd normally use curry powder. It's especially good in seafood stews and potato salads.

$1/3$ cup coriander seeds	2 teaspoons anise seeds
2 tablespoons cumin seeds	1 teaspoon fennel seeds
8 cardamom pods	1 cinnamon stick, $1/2$ inch long
5 whole cloves	1 pea-size chip of fresh nutmeg
2 tablespoons sesame seeds	2 bay leaves
1 tablespoon black peppercorns	

Combine the coriander, cumin, cardamom, cloves, sesame seeds, peppercorns, anise seeds, fennel, cinnamon, nutmeg, and bay leaves in a dry skillet and cook over medium heat, shaking the pan, until the spices are lightly toasted and fragrant, about 3 minutes. Alternatively, the spices can be roasted in the oven. Transfer the spices to a bowl to cool.

Place the spices in a spice mill and grind to a fine powder.

Store the mixture in an airtight container away from light. It will keep for several months.

Makes $1\frac{1}{2}$ cups.

Cuban Adobo

ADOBO IS USED IN ONE FORM or another throughout the Spanish Caribbean. But nowhere does it play as central a role as it does in the cooking of Cuba. There aren't many Cuban dishes—be they pork, beef, chicken, or seafood—that aren't marinated in this lively blend of garlic, cumin, and citrus juice prior to frying, sautéing, roasting, baking, or grilling.

In Cuba, the citrus fruit of choice for this recipe would be the sour orange (*naranja agria*), a fruit that looks like a lumpy orange but tastes more like a lime. Sour oranges (which are similar to Europe's Seville orange) are sold at Hispanic and West Indian markets. If unavailable, fresh lime juice makes a perfectly delectable adobo. Indeed, many Cubans use lime juice instead of sour orange juice.

6 to 8 garlic cloves, coarsely chopped

2 teaspoons salt, or to taste

1 teaspoon ground cumin

1 teaspoon dried oregano

1 teaspoon freshly ground black pepper

¼ teaspoon ground bay leaves (optional)

⅔ cup fresh sour orange juice
   or lime juice

Place the garlic, salt, cumin, oregano, black pepper, and bay leaves in a mortar and pestle and mash to a fine paste. Work in the sour orange juice or lime juice. Alternatively, place all the ingredients in a blender and puree. Correct the seasoning, adding salt or cumin to taste.

Store the mixture in a jar in the refrigerator. It will keep for up to a week, but it tastes best when used within a day or two.

Makes about ¾ cup—enough Adobo for 1½ pounds of meat, chicken, or seafood.

NOTE: Adobo is the marinade used to make Cuba's famous *lechon asado*, roast suckling pig. You'll need to quadruple or quintuple this recipe for a 20-pound pig. Adobo also makes an uncommonly succulent roast turkey.

MARINATING TIMES FOR ADOBO

➤ Whole chicken or turkey (put some of the Adobo in the cavity, some under the skin, and rub the rest over the skin)	12 hours
➤ Whole pork roasts or tenderloins	4 to 8 hours
➤ Rack of lamb and beef tenderloins	4 to 8 hours
➤ Whole fish (put some of the Adobo in the cavity, some in slits in the flesh, and pour the rest over the skin)	2 to 4 hours
➤ Chicken breasts, steaks, pork chops	1 hour
➤ Shrimp and fish fillets	½ to 1 hour

Montego bay meets memphis in this recipe, a spice rub based on Jamaica's traditional jerk seasoning. Sprinkle this rub on ribs, pork chops, chicken breasts, and seafood prior to grilling. Or substitute it for Cajun spice in your favorite pan-blackening recipe. You can also stir a few tablespoons into sour cream to make an unusual dip.

The traditional chili pepper for jerk is, of course, the Jamaican hot or Scotch bonnet. This recipe calls for the closely related habanero chili, which is more readily available dried or powdered.

When grinding whole dried habaneros, drape a dish towel over the grinder or blender and take care not to inhale the dust. Several companies sell habanero chili powder. I've suggested a range for the chili powder: the tender of tongue should start with 1 tablespoon; the pyromaniac will want to use the full 2.

OPPOSITE
*Red Snapper seasoned
with Dry Jerk Seasoning*

1 to 2 tablespoons habanero chili powder,
  or to taste

¼ cup freeze-dried chives

2 tablespoons onion powder

2 tablespoons garlic powder

2 tablespoons kosher salt

4 teaspoons ground coriander

4 teaspoons ground ginger

2 teaspoons freshly ground black pepper

2 teaspoons dried thyme

2 teaspoons ground allspice

1 teaspoon ground cinnamon

½ teaspoon ground cloves

½ teaspoon freshly grated nutmeg

Combine the chili powder, chives, onion powder, garlic powder, salt, coriander, ginger, pepper, thyme, allspice, cinnamon, cloves, and nutmeg in a spice mill or blender and grind to a fine powder.

Store the rub in a jar or airtight box away from heat and light. It will keep for several months.

Makes about 1 cup.

Rasta Rings

T HESE AREN'T YOUR RUN-OF-THE-MILL ONION RINGS, not with their fiery seasoning of Volcanic Hot Sauce (page 58) and Jamaican Dry Jerk Seasoning. The buttermilk makes the onion rings exceptionally tender. Rasta Rings would make a good accompaniment to the Palomilla on page 46.

2 large white onions (about 1 pound)

2½ cups buttermilk

1 to 2 tablespoons Volcanic Hot Sauce
  (page 58), or your favorite hot sauce

1 cup all-purpose flour

1 cup fine white cornmeal

2 tablespoons cornstarch

⅓ cup Dry Jerk Seasoning (page 29)

1 tablespoon salt, plus salt for sprinkling

2 to 3 cups canola oil

Peel the onions and cut crosswise into thin (⅛- to ¼-inch) slices. Break the slices into rings with your fingers and place them in a shallow bowl with the buttermilk and hot sauce. Gently toss to mix and place in the refrigerator. Marinate the onion rings in this mixture for 1 to 2 hours, mixing as necessary.

Combine the flour, cornmeal, cornstarch, ¼ cup jerk seasoning, and 1 tablespoon salt in another mixing bowl and whisk to mix.

Just before serving, heat 1½ to 2 inches of oil to 375°F. in a skillet or electric frying pan.

Remove the onion rings from the buttermilk and drain. Toss the rings in the seasoned flour. Remove the rings from the flour, shaking off the excess, and lower them into the oil. Fry the onion rings until golden brown, 1 to 2 minutes, working in several batches. Transfer the onion rings to paper towels to drain. Sprinkle the Rasta Rings with the remaining jerk seasoning, salt to taste, and serve at once.

Serves 4.

Wet Jerk Seasoning

Jerk is Jamaica's most famous dish, and it has taken the world by storm. The preparation originated, so the story goes, with the Maroons, or runaway slaves, who would season boar and other wild game with a fiery paste of chives, allspice, and Scotch bonnet chilies to help prevent it from spoiling. The meat would be smoked over a pimento (allspice) wood fire.

Today, the term *jerk* refers to the seasoning, the style of cooking, and the finished dish. (The same is true of the American word *barbecue*.) Jerk pork and jerk chicken have become staples not only in Jamaica but throughout North America, while adventurous cooks are experimenting with everything from jerk rabbit to jerk pasta.

When jerking meat, it's customary to make tiny holes in the meat with the tip of a knife and rub a little Jerk Seasoning in each hole. In addition to its use as a marinade for grilled fare, this Jerk Seasoning makes a wonderful addition to scrambled eggs, mashed potatoes, and sour-cream based dips.

Warning: Scotch bonnet chilies are fiendishly fiery. Wear gloves when handling Scotch bonnets and be sure not to touch your eyes or face until you've thoroughly washed your hands. Take care not to breathe in the fumes when you uncover the blender. If you're not used to them, there are three ways to attenuate the heat in this recipe—use fewer Scotch bonnets, seed them, or substitute a milder chili, like a jalapeño. Twelve Scotch bonnet chilies will give you the heat of an authentic jerk marinade.

2 to 12 Scotch bonnet chilies, stemmed

1 medium onion, coarsely chopped

4 to 5 shallots, coarsely chopped (about ¼ cup)

2 bunches of chives or scallions, trimmed to remove the roots and coarsely chopped

1 cup coarsely chopped fresh flat-leaf parsley

4 garlic cloves, coarsely chopped

1 tablespoon finely chopped fresh ginger

3 tablespoons salt, or to taste

2 teaspoons chopped fresh thyme (or dried)

2 teaspoons ground allspice

1 teaspoon freshly ground black pepper

½ teaspoon freshly grated nutmeg

¼ teaspoon ground cinnamon

⅛ teaspoon ground cloves

¼ cup fresh lime juice or distilled white vinegar

3 tablespoons soy sauce

2 tablespoons vegetable oil

1 tablespoon brown sugar

2 tablespoons water or as needed

Combine the chilies, onion, shallots, chives, parsley, and garlic in a food processor and puree to a coarse paste. Work in the ginger, salt, thyme, allspice, black pepper, nutmeg, cinnamon, cloves, lime juice, soy sauce, vegetable oil, and brown sugar. Correct the seasoning, adding soy sauce or salt to taste as needed. The mixture should be very flavorful. Add water as needed to obtain a thick but pourable paste.

Makes 1½ cups—enough Jerk Seasoning for 2 pounds meat, chicken, or seafood.

NOTE: The ingredients can also be pureed in the blender. Add all the ingredients at once. Store the Jerk Seasoning in a glass jar with a nonreactive lid. (Or cover the jar with plastic wrap, then screw on the lid. This prevents the jerk seasoning from corroding a metal lid.) Refrigerated, Jerk Seasoning will keep for several weeks or even months. Of course, the sooner you use it, the better it will taste.

MARINATING TIMES FOR JERK

➤ Whole chicken (put some of the seasoning in the cavity, some under the skin, and rub the rest over the skin)	12 to 24 hours
➤ Whole pork shoulders or tenderloins (make tiny holes in the meat with the tip of a knife and rub a little of the seasoning in each hole)	12 to 24 hours
➤ Rack of lamb and beef tenderloins (make tiny holes in the meat with the tip of a knife and rub a little of the seasoning in each hole)	12 to 24 hours
➤ Whole fish (put some of the seasoning in the cavity, some in slits in the flesh, and rub the rest over the skin)	4 to 6 hours
➤ Chicken breasts, steaks, pork chops, tofu	2 to 4 hours
➤ Shrimp and fish fillets	½ to 1 hour

Seasonin'

It's hard to imagine a bajan (barbadian) recipe that doesn't begin with Seasonin'. This tongue-tingling paste of garlic, chives, peppers, and chilies is the obligatory seasoning for poultry, meats, and seafood. It's just the thing for perking up a lackluster soup or stew. Indeed, a tablespoon or two can have an invigorating effect on just about any dish to which you add it.

Although Seasonin' contains a Scotch bonnet chili, it isn't unbearably hot. It's the perfect condiment for people who find Jamaican Dry Jerk Seasoning (see page 29) too fiery. For information about how to handle Scotch bonnets, see page 32.

The West Indian chive tastes like a cross between a scallion and a shallot. If unavailable, use fresh regular chives or scallions. This recipes was inspired by a gifted chef and dear friend from Barbados, Sharon Morrisson.

1 head garlic, broken into cloves and peeled (10 to 12 cloves)

1 medium onion, halved and coarsely chopped

3 bunches of chives or 2 bunches of scallions, trimmed and coarsely chopped

1 green bell pepper, cored, seeded, and coarsely chopped

½ red bell pepper, cored, seeded, and coarsely chopped

1 celery stalk

1 Scotch bonnet or 2 jalapeño peppers, seeded and minced (for hotter Seasonin' leave the seeds in)

1 bunch of flat-leaf parsley, stemmed and coarsely chopped (about 1 cup)

1 bunch of fresh thyme, stemmed, or 1 tablespoon dried

1 bunch of fresh marjoram, stemmed, or 1 tablespoon dried (optional)

½ cup fresh lime juice (3 to 4 limes)

Salt and freshly ground black pepper

Coarsely puree the garlic, onion, bell peppers, celery, chili peppers, chives, herbs, and lime juice in a food processor or pound to a paste in a mortar and pestle. Correct the seasoning, adding salt and pepper or lime juice to taste. The mixture should be very flavorful.

Store Seasonin' in a glass jar with a nonreactive lid. Refrigerated, it will keep for several weeks. Of course, the sooner you use it, the better it will taste.

Makes 2½ cups—enough for 2 pounds of meat, chicken, or seafood.

MARINATING TIMES FOR SEASONIN'

➤ Whole chicken (put some of the Seasonin' in the cavity, some under the skin, and rub the rest over the skin)	12 to 24 hours
➤ Whole pork shoulders or tenderloins	8 to 12 hours
➤ Whole fish (put some of the Seasonin' in the cavity, some in slits in the flesh, and rub the rest over the skin)	4 to 6 hours
➤ Chicken breasts, steaks, pork chops, tofu	2 to 4 hours
➤ Shrimp and fish fillets	1 to 2 hours

THIS IS A GREAT DISH FOR ENTERTAINING. The hens are flavored with a tangy Bajan herb paste called Seasonin'. To maximize moistness and flavor, part of the Seasonin' is spread under the hens' skins. This procedure isn't particularly difficult, but it may take a little practice.

Bajan Roast Chicken would be prepared the same way.

4 Cornish game hens (1¼ to
  1½ pounds each)
Salt and freshly ground black pepper

About 1 cup Seasonin' (page 34)
2 tablespoons butter or olive oil

Remove any lumps of fat from inside the birds. Season the cavities with salt and pepper and place 1 tablespoon Seasonin' in each. Preheat the oven to 400°F.

Starting at the neck of each bird, worm your finger under the skin to create a pocket between the skin and the breast meat. Try to loosen the skin over the breast, thighs, and drumsticks. Work carefully so as not to tear the skin. This will feel a little strange at first, but you'll get the hang of it with practice.

Spread 2 tablespoons Seasonin' under the skin of each bird. (This is most easily done with a small spoon.) Tightly truss each bird with string. Season the outside of the birds with salt and pepper. Transfer the hens, breast side up, to a roasting pan with a rack. Spoon the remaining Seasonin' on top of the birds and place ½ tablespoon butter on each.

Roast the birds for 30 to 40 minutes, or until golden brown. To test for doneness, insert a trussing needle into the thickest part of the thigh. The juices will run clear when the bird is cooked. Transfer the birds to a platter and let stand for 3 minutes. Remove the trussing string and serve at once.

Serves 4.

Paramin Seasoning

As is the case throughout the southern Caribbean, the first step in many Trinidadian recipes is to prepare a batch of seasoning. This tangy herb marinade seems to enhance the flavor of any meat or fish it touches. The most famous seasoning in Trinidad comes from the town of Paramin, a hilltop community a half-hour north of Port of Spain.

Paramin is Trinidad's herb basket: its steep hillsides are planted with patches of parsley, thyme, mint, West Indian chives, and an herb that's one of the defining flavors of Trinidadian cooking: *chandon beni* (literally "false cilantro"). Known as *culentro* in English, *chandon beni* is a flat, thumb-shaped, sawtooth-edged herb that tastes like strong cilantro with a slightly bitter aftertaste. Look for culentro at Hispanic or West Indian markets or substitute fresh cilantro.

To round out Paramin Seasoning, Trinidadians use a chili pepper called a seasoning pepper, which tastes like a Scotch bonnet without the heat. Possible substitutes in the United States include green bell pepper, cachucha pepper (a small, pattypan squash–shaped chili sometimes called rocotillo pepper or *aji dulce*), or even a seeded, deveined Scotch bonnet.

4 scallions, trimmed

2 shallots or ½ small onion, coarsely chopped

2 garlic cloves, coarsely chopped

1 celery stalk, coarsely chopped

1 bunch of culentro or cilantro, washed, stemmed, and coarsely chopped

½ cup washed, stemmed, fresh flat-leaf parsley leaves

¼ cup fresh mint leaves

1 tablespoon chopped fresh or dried thyme

4 cachucha peppers, ¼ green bell pepper, or ½ Scotch bonnet, seeded and deveined

⅓ cup lime juice (2 to 3 limes)

1 tablespoon salt

1 teaspoon freshly ground black pepper

Combine the ingredients in a blender or processor, add 1 cup water, and blend to a loose puree. If using a food processor, puree the scallions, shallots, garlic, celery, culentro, parsley, mint, thyme, peppers, and salt first, then add the lime juice and water. Correct the seasoning, adding more lime juice or salt and pepper to taste.

Store the seasoning in a jar in the refrigerator. It will keep for up to 2 weeks.

Makes about 2 cups—enough seasoning for 2 pounds meat, chicken, or seafood.

MARINATING TIMES FOR PARAMIN SEASONING

➤ Whole chicken or turkey (put some of the seasoning in the cavity, some under the skin, and rub the rest over the skin)	12 hours
➤ Whole pork roasts or tenderloins	6 to 8 hours
➤ Rack of lamb and beef tenderloins	6 to 8 hours
➤ Whole fish (put some of the seasoning in the cavity, some in slits in the flesh, and pour the rest over the skin)	3 to 6 hours
➤ Chicken breasts, steaks, pork chops	2 hours
➤ Shrimp and fish fillets	1 hour

Recado (Orange Annatto Marinade from the Yucatan)

THIS RECIPE TAKES US TO THE YUCATAN in the western corner of the Caribbean. Recado is easy to make, but you need to know about two special ingredients: annatto seed and sour orange.

Annatto is a rust-colored seed with a mild, earthy flavor. It's sometimes sold by the name *achiote*. Look for it at Hispanic and West Indian markets and many supermarkets, especially ones with a large Hispanic clientele. Sour orange looks like an orange but tastes like a lime (see page 26).

Recado goes particularly well with seafood, chicken, and pork.

1 teaspoon annatto seeds

1 cup fresh sweet orange juice

1/2 cup sour orange juice or fresh lime juice

2 tablespoons wine vinegar

1 medium onion, quartered

2 shallots, halved

10 garlic cloves

2 tablespoons paprika

1 tablespoon fresh oregano

1 teaspoon lightly toasted cumin seeds or ground cumin

10 black peppercorns

2 allspice berries

2 whole cloves

2 teaspoons salt, or to taste

Soak the annatto seeds in the citrus juices and vinegar for 30 minutes or until soft. Preheat a broiler or grill.

Broil or grill the onion, shallots, and garlic on a piece of foil until nicely browned on the outside and tender inside, about 5 minutes, turning as necessary. Transfer the vegetables to a platter and let cool.

Combine the annatto seeds with their soaking liquid, the grilled vegetables, spices, and seasonings in a blender and blend to a smooth paste. (The blender works better than the food processor for this purpose.) Correct the seasoning, adding salt or more lime juice or orange juice to taste. The mixture should be very flavorful.

You can store Recado in the refrigerator for up to 1 week.

Makes 2 cups—enough for 2 pounds of pork, chicken, or seafood. For the best results, cook the food on a grill.

MARINATING TIMES FOR RECADO

➤ Whole chicken (put some of the Recado in the cavity, some under the skin, and rub the rest over the skin)	6 hours
➤ Whole pork roasts or tenderloins	6 hours
➤ Whole fish (put some of the Recado in the cavity, some in slits in the flesh, and pour the rest over the skin)	3 hours
➤ Chicken breasts or pork chops	1 to 2 hours
➤ Shrimp and fish fillets	½ hour

MILD SAUCES AND HOT SAUCES

Mojo (Cuban Garlic-Cumin-Citrus Sauce)

OPPOSITE
Palomilla (page 46)

Mojo—PRONOUNCED—"MO-HO"—IS TO CUBA what salsa is to Mexico. This tart table sauce—redolent of garlic and cumin—is splashed on everything from sandwiches to steamed vegetables to grilled fish and steak.

A Cuban would use the acidic juice of the *naranja agria* (sour orange) in his mojo. Sour oranges look like bumpy greenish-orange oranges and can sometimes be found at Hispanic grocery stores. But excellent mojo can be made with fresh lime juice, which is much more readily available.

Hispanic markets and a growing number of supermarkets carry commercial bottled mojos. But the sauce is easy to make at home and the results are a lot tastier.

½ cup olive oil

6 to 8 large garlic cloves, cut into paper-thin slices or finely chopped

⅔ cup fresh lime or sour orange juice

1 teaspoon ground cumin

½ teaspoon dried oregano

2 teaspoons salt, or to taste

1 teaspoon freshly ground black pepper

3 tablespoons chopped fresh cilantro or flat-leaf parsley

Heat the olive oil in a deep saucepan over medium heat. Add the garlic and cook until fragrant and a pale golden brown. Do not let brown too much, or the garlic will become bitter.

Stir in the lime juice, ½ cup water, cumin, oregano, salt, and pepper. Stand back; the sauce may sputter. Bring the sauce to a rolling boil. Correct the seasoning, adding salt and pepper to taste. Let cool to room temperature, then stir in the cilantro.

Store Mojo in a glass bottle in the refrigerator. It will keep for several weeks. (Of course, it tastes best served within a few hours.) Shake well before using.

Makes 1½ cups.

Palomilla (Cuban Marinated Shell Steak Served with Onions and Mojo)

See photograph on page 45

Palomilla is a dish from Cuban cowboy country: steak marinated in adobo, the ubiquitous Cuban seasoning made with garlic, cumin, and sour orange juice. These flavors are reinforced by the garlicky mojo sauce. The preparation of adobo is fully described on page 26, of mojo on page 44.

The traditional topping for palomilla is thinly sliced raw onion. I've added a modern touch—grilled onion—in the following recipe, but you can always go back to tradition. Chicken or seafood can be prepared the same way, but decrease the marinating time.

4 (8- to 10-ounce) shell steaks (also known
   as ribeyes)
1 cup Cuban Adobo (page 26)
1 tablespoon olive oil

1 to 2 medium onions, cut crosswise
   into ½-inch slices
¼ cup Mojo (page 44)

Marinate the steaks in the Cuban Adobo in a nonreactive baking dish for 30 minutes, turning several times.

Preheat a grill to high. Remove the steaks from the marinade and blot dry. Lightly brush steaks with olive oil. Grill the steaks until cooked to taste (2 to 3 minutes per side for medium-rare). Brush the onion slices with the remaining olive oil and grill them until nicely browned, 2 to 3 minutes per side, turning with a spatula.

Transfer the steaks to plates or a platter and top with grilled onions. Spoon the Mojo on top and serve at once.

Serves 4.

Ajilimojili (Puerto Rican Cilantro Sauce)

Pronounced a-HE-lee-mo-HE-lee, ajilimojili belongs to an illustrious family of Caribbean table sauces that includes Cuban mojo (see page 44) and French West Indian *Sauce Chien* (see page 49).

To be strictly authentic, you'd need two special ingredients: *aji dulce* peppers and culentro. The former (known by Cubans as *chili cachucha*) is a tiny, pattypan squash–shaped pepper that hints at the floral fragrance of the Scotch bonnet but without the latter's tongue-torturing heat.

Culentro is a finger-size, dark green, flat-leaf herb with a distinctive sawtooth edge. Its pungent flavor is similar to that of cilantro but a little more bitter. Both *aji dulce* and culentro are available at Hispanic markets. But a perfectly tasty ajilimojili can be made using red bell pepper in place of the *aji dulce* and a little more cilantro instead of the culentro.

Traditionally served over *tostones* (fried mashed green plantains) and boiled vegetables, Ajilimojili makes a delectable accompaniment to grilled seafood, vegetables, and especially grilled meats. You can also use it as a marinade. You can even mix a few tablespoons of Ajilimojili with mashed avocado to make a Puerto Rican–style guacamole.

The following recipe was inspired by one of the foremost authorities on Puerto Rican cooking, author, columnist, and television chef Giovanna Huyke.

2 medium onions, quartered
5 garlic cloves
1 green bell pepper, cored, seeded, and diced
12 cachucha peppers, stemmed and seeded, or
  3 tablespoons diced red bell pepper
1 bunch of fresh cilantro, washed and stemmed

5 culentro leaves (or a little
  more cilantro)
1 teaspoon dried oregano
1 cup extra-virgin olive oil
1/2 cup red wine vinegar
Salt and freshly ground black pepper

Puree the onions, garlic, peppers, cilantro, culentro, and oregano in a food processor. Add the olive oil, vinegar, salt, and pepper and puree until smooth. Correct the seasoning, adding more salt or vinegar to taste.

The sauce can also be made in the blender. In this case, add all the ingredients at once.

Transfer the sauce to clean glass jars. Refrigerated, it will keep several weeks. (Of course, it's better served sooner than later.)

Makes 3 cups.

St. Barts Creole Sauce

WHENEVER I RETURN TO ST. BARTHÉLEMY, my first stop usually is the Marigot Bay Club. I want to see if the grilled creole lobster is really as good as I remember it. (It always is.) This open-air restaurant sits right on the tiny beach at Marigot Bay. If the water were any closer, you'd have to dine in your bathing suit.

Marigot Bay Club owner Michel Ledee is an avid fisherman. His boat is a genuine Maine lobster boat brought down from the United States. For years I've pestered Michel for the recipe for his wonderful creole sauce. We finally agreed on a swap: my conch fritters for his creole sauce.

Creole Sauce is great with grilled lobster, shrimp, fish, and other seafood. Use it as a dip for fritters or even in place of cocktail sauce for oysters and shrimp.

2 tablespoons unsalted butter

1 small onion, finely chopped (about ½ cup)

3 scallions, trimmed and finely chopped

2 garlic cloves, minced

2 tablespoons chopped fresh flat-leaf parsley

2 teaspoons fresh thyme

1 cup tomato ketchup

1 tablespoon wine vinegar

1 tablespoon lime juice

1 teaspoon honey (optional)

½ to 1 teaspoon Caribbean hot sauce (such as the Volcanic Hot Sauce on page 58)

Salt and freshly ground black pepper

Melt the butter in a saucepan. Add the onion, scallions, garlic, parsley, and thyme and cook over medium heat until soft, about 3 minutes. Stir in the ketchup, vinegar, lime juice, honey if using, hot sauce, salt and pepper, and ½ cup water. Bring the sauce to a boil, then reduce the heat and gently simmer for 3 minutes. Correct the seasoning, adding more hot sauce, lime juice, or salt to taste.

Transfer the sauce to a clean jar. Refrigerated, it will keep for up to 2 weeks.

Makes 2 cups.

SAUCE CHIEN IS A SORT OF HIGH-VOLTAGE VINAIGRETTE served as a table sauce in the French West Indies. There are several theories as to just how the sauce got its curious name, literally "dog sauce."

According to one theory, the name suggests the bite of its primary ingredients: garlic and Scotch bonnet chilies (see page 32). Another holds that "dog" reflects the sauce's humble status within the French repertory. After all, *Sauce Chien* can be made in a matter of minutes and it lacks the egg yolks, butter, and cream found in the so-called noble French sauces, such as hollandaise or beurre blanc.

Whatever its origins, *Sauce Chien* is an indispensable accompaniment to grilled seafood, chicken, and vegetables throughout the French islands. The addition of boiling water helps mellow the bite of the raw garlic and chives.

2 garlic cloves, minced

$1/2$ teaspoon salt, or to taste

$1/2$ to 1 Scotch bonnet chili, seeded and minced (for a hotter sauce leave the seeds in)

1 shallot, minced

2 tablespoons finely chopped fresh chives or scallion greens

2 tablespoons finely chopped fresh cilantro (optional)

2 tablespoons finely chopped fresh flat-leaf parsley

$1/2$ teaspoon chopped fresh thyme

Freshly ground black pepper to taste

3 tablespoon fresh lime juice, or to taste

$1/4$ cup extra-virgin olive oil

3 to 4 tablespoons boiling water

Mash the garlic and salt to a smooth paste with a fork in the bottom of a mixing bowl. Whisk in the chili, shallot, chives, cilantro, parsley, thyme, black pepper, and lime juice. Whisk in the oil in a thin stream. Add a few tablespoons (3 to 4 as needed) of boiling water to obtain a pourable, mellow-tasting sauce. Correct the seasoning, adding more salt or lime juice to taste.

Sauce Chien can be served at once, but the flavor will improve if it is allowed to stand for 1 hour. Transfer it to a clean jar with a nonreactive lid. Spoon the sauce over grilled fish, chicken, and lamb, or use in salads, soups, and steamed or grilled vegetables.

Sauce Chien will keep for up to 1 week in the refrigerator, but is best served the same day. Shake or whisk it before using.

Makes 1 cup.

Plantain, Sweet Potato, and Mesclun Salad with *Sauce Chien*

THIS COLORFUL SALAD features a quintessential caribbean vegetable—plantain—plus a vinaigrettelike table sauce prized throughout the French West Indies, *sauce chien.*

Plantain is a cooking banana, a jumbo cousin of the fruit we slice onto breakfast cereal. Unlike regular banana, plantain is always served cooked. A green plantain is starchy and not at all sweet—it reminds me of a potato. Ripe plantain has the fruity sweetness of a banana while retaining a pleasing acidity as well. To ripen a green plantain, leave it at room temperature for four to six days, or until the skin is yellow and black. Plantains can be found in Hispanic and West Indian markets and most supermarkets.

This recipe was inspired by a dish I tasted at the restaurant Au Port in Gustavia, St. Barthélemy.

2 orange sweet potatoes (choose long slender potatoes, 8 to 10 ounces each)

1 ripe plantain

4 cups mesclun (mixed baby greens), washed and dried

6 tablespoons *Sauce Chien* (page 49)

Freshly ground black pepper

Preheat the oven to 400°F. Prick the sweet potatoes and plantain in a few spots with a fork. Place the vegetables on a baking sheet and roast for 1 hour or until tender. (They should be easy to pierce with a skewer.) Transfer the vegetables to a plate to cool. Peel the sweet potatoes and plantain and cut each crosswise into ¼-inch slices. If you're in a hurry, you can steam the vegetables until tender, about 15 minutes.

Arrange the sweet potato and plantain slices in a circle around the outer edge of four salad plates, overlapping sweet potato and plantain to create a colorful border. In a mixing bowl gently toss the mesclun with 3 tablespoons *Sauce Chien.* Mound the mesclun in the center of each plate. Drizzle the remaining sauce over the sweet potato and plantain. Sprinkle the salads with freshly ground black pepper and serve at once.

Serves 4.

Pindasaus (Indonesian-Style Peanut Sauce)

SOME OF THE BEST FOOD IN THE ÐUTCH WEST INDIES is neither Dutch nor West Indian. Consider this peanut sauce, the traditional accompaniment to the Indonesian kebabs known as satays. This recipe bears tribute to the deep roots of the East Indies in the southern Caribbean, particularly on the island of Curaçao. After all, this island (the largest of the Dutch Antilles) was originally settled by the Dutch East Indies Trading Company—the same company that opened Western trade with what eventually became Indonesia. The cross-cultural exchange between these two regions continues to this day.

This recipe was inspired by the Indonesia Rijstafel restaurant in Willemstad, where it's served as part of a traditional rijstafel (pronounced RICE-tafel), literally "rice table"—a belt-loosening array of kebabs, stews, salads, and condiments (as many as twenty-six different dishes in all) served around a centerpiece of steamed rice.

The special ingredients called for in this recipe are discussed in the notes below.

¼ cup finely chopped onion

1 garlic clove, minced

1 teaspoon *sambal ulek* (see Note)

¾ cup peanut butter

3 tablespoons Tamarind Water (page 118)

2 to 3 tablespoons *kejap manis* (see Note) or soy sauce

2 tablespoons distilled white vinegar

½ to 1 cup chicken stock or water

Place the onion, garlic, and *sambal* in a mortar and pestle and pound to a smooth paste. (Alternatively, place them in a large bowl and mash with the back of a wooden spoon.) Stir in the peanut butter, followed by the remaining ingredients. Transfer the mixture to a heavy saucepan.

Place the pan over medium heat and gently simmer the sauce for 5 minutes or until well flavored, adding more water as necessary to obtain a thick but pourable sauce.

Transfer the sauce to a clear glass jar. Refrigerated, it will keep for up to 4 weeks.

Pindasaus is traditionally served with pork and chicken satays, but it's also delicious as a salad dressing or a dip for raw or steamed vegetables.

Stored in a clean jar in the refrigerator, it will keep for up to 2 weeks.

Makes 1½ cups.

NOTE: You'll need to know about three special ingredients to prepare this recipe: *sambal ulek*, *ketjap manis*, and tamarind water. *Sambal ulek* is a fiery paste made of red peppers. Look for it in gourmet shops or Asian markets, or use a Vietnamese or Thai chili paste or even the Volcanic Hot Sauce on page 58. *Ketjap manis*, a forerunner of our ketchup, is a thick, sweet soy sauce. Again, look for it at Asian markets or substitute equal parts regular soy sauce and molasses. Tamarind Water is explained in full on page 118. If unavailable, substitute balsamic vinegar.

Mamba (Haitian Peanut Sauce)

THIS TANGY SAUCE REFLECTS THE AFRO-CARIBBEAN fondness for peanuts. The recipe came to me via Time magazine bureau chief Cathy Booth from the Cardozo sisters, proprietors of the Hotel Montana in the Port-au-Prince suburb of Pétionville. The Haitian pepper is a cousin of the Scotch bonnet, an elongated wrinkled chili pepper hot enough to weld your tongue to the roof of your mouth. The Cardozo sisters aren't as fond of these chilies as many of their compatriots are, so I've made them optional.

Mamba is traditionally served with chicken, beef, or seafood. It makes a great sauce for grilled or steamed vegetables and an original dip for crudités.

1 tablespoon olive oil

1 small onion, finely chopped

3 garlic cloves, minced

½ to 1 Haitian or Scotch bonnet pepper, seeded and minced (optional; see page 32)

½ cup chunky peanut butter

1 cup chicken or beef stock, or as needed

1 teaspoon fresh lime juice

2 tablespoons chopped fresh flat-leaf parsley

Salt and freshly ground black pepper

Heat the olive oil in a heavy saucepan. Add the onion, garlic, and pepper and cook over medium heat until just beginning to brown, about 5 minutes.

Add the peanut butter and stock and simmer, whisking or stirring, until well blended; add more stock as necessary to achieve a pourable sauce. Stir in the lime juice and parsley. Correct the seasoning, adding salt and plenty of black pepper to taste.

Mamba will keep for 10 days in the refrigerator, but you'll need to stir it before serving. Makes 1 cup.

Sofrito

Sofrito is the cornerstone—some might say the very soul—of Spanish Caribbean cooking. Walk into a Hispanic home and you're likely to smell the comforting aroma of sautéed onions, garlic, and peppers. Taste any of the soulful stews of the Spanish Caribbean—from Cuban *enchilado* to Puerto Rican *asopao*—and you're sure to experience the evocative flavors of a preparation that's as old as the Spanish presence in the New World.

The recipe for sofrito varies from cook to cook and island to island. The basic ingredients include onion, garlic, and peppers. Some cooks use red bell peppers, others green, and still others prefer the aromatic flavor of the tiny cachucha pepper (also known as rocotillo pepper and *aji dulce*). Optional ingredients can include tomatoes, cilantro, and salt pork. Traditionally these ingredients would have been sautéed in lard, but today health-conscious cooks have switched to olive oil.

Cubans favor a red sofrito made with red bell peppers and tomatoes and scented with cumin, oregano, and bay leaf. Puerto Ricans prefer green sofrito, also called *recaito*, which is built from green bell, rocotillo, or cubanelle peppers, onion, cilantro, and sometimes culentro. A little bacon or salt pork is often added to a Puerto Rican sofrito.

Following are a Cuban-style Red Sofrito and a Puerto Rican-style Green Sofrito. The green is especially good in seafood dishes, where a red sofrito might be overpowering. Add capers and olives to the Green Sofrito and you get Salsa Verde, a popular accompaniment to fish throughout the Spanish Caribbean.

Use either sofrito as a starting point for soups, stews, and rice dishes. Add it to your favorite tomato sauce for truly memorable spaghetti. You can even spread it on toast points or crostini to make an offbeat appetizer.

Red Sofrito

2 tablespoons olive oil

1 medium onion, finely chopped (about 1 cup)

1 red bell pepper, cored, seeded, and finely diced (about 1 cup)

3 garlic cloves, minced

3/4 teaspoon cumin, or to taste

1/2 teaspoon dried oregano

1 bay leaf

1 ripe tomato, finely chopped

1/2 teaspoon salt

Freshly ground black pepper to taste

Heat the olive oil in a nonstick frying pan or sauté pan. Add the onion, pepper, garlic, cumin, oregano, and bay leaf. Cook over medium heat until soft and translucent but not brown, about 5 minutes, stirring with a wooden spoon.

Add the tomato, salt, and pepper. Continue cooking the Sofrito until the tomato juices have evaporated and the mixture is intensely aromatic, about 5 minutes. Correct the seasoning, adding salt or cumin to taste.

Transfer the Sofrito to a clean glass jar. Refrigerated, it will keep for up to a week.

Makes 1½ cups.

Green Sofrito/Salsa Verde

2 tablespoons olive oil
1 very small onion, finely chopped (about ½ cup)
1 bunch of scallions, trimmed and finely chopped
4 garlic cloves, minced
1 green bell pepper, cored, seeded, and finely chopped

¼ cup chopped fresh cilantro
¼ cup chopped fresh flat-leaf parsley
4 culentro leaves, finely chopped (optional; see page 38)
½ teaspoon salt, or to taste
Freshly ground black pepper to taste

Heat the olive oil in a nonstick frying pan or sauté pan. Add the onion, scallions, garlic, and bell pepper. Cook over medium heat until soft and translucent but not brown, about 5 minutes, stirring with a wooden spoon.

Stir in the cilantro, parsley, culentro, salt, and pepper. Cook the mixture for a minute or two longer. Correct the seasoning, adding more salt and pepper to taste.

Transfer the sofrito to a clean glass jar. Refrigerated, it will keep for up to a week.

Makes 1 cup.

NOTE: To make Salsa Verde, mince ¼ cup flat-leaf parsley as finely as possible. Wrap the parsley in a clean dishcloth. Tightly twist the cloth to wring out the parsley juice into the salsa. (This gives the sauce a rich green hue.) Stir in 1 tablespoon of finely chopped capers, 1 tablespoon chopped pitted green olives, and 1 tablespoon butter and cook for 1 minute more. Salsa Verde makes a great accompaniment to grilled seafood. Refrigerated in a clean glass jar, it will keep for about 1 week.

EVERY COUNTRY IN THE CARIBBEAN has its preferred hot sauce, a devilish liquid deemed essential to the proper enjoyment of a meal. I know of a Bahamian grandfather, for example, who would never leave his home without a flask of this fiery condiment in his pocket.

Bahamians dote on sherry peppers—dry sherry ignited with bird peppers or tongue-torturing Scotch bonnets. It's hard to imagine a Bahamian conch chowder or Scotched conch without a few drops of this electrifying elixir. The sherry reveals the islands' British heritage. A similar preparation is made in Barbados, where it is called pepper wine.

There are two possibilities for peppers here: the bird pepper, a small, slender, bright red member of the cayenne family; or the infamous Scotch bonnet. (See page 32 for information on how to handle Scotch bonnets.)

½ to 1 cup bird peppers or Scotch bonnets
1 bottle sherry (preferably amontillado)

Stem the peppers and wash thoroughly. If using bird peppers, leave them whole. If using Scotch bonnets, cut each pepper lengthwise into quarters.

Pour 1 cup sherry out of the bottle into a measuring cup. Place the peppers in the bottle. Top up the bottle with the remaining sherry. Tightly cap the bottle.

Let the sherry peppers steep for at least 2 weeks, preferably a month, before serving. To use, sprinkle a few drops into soups, stews, conch chowder, or any dish in need of a little fire.

Sherry peppers will keep almost indefinitely at room temperature.

Makes 1 bottle.

Pepper Rum

SIMILAR IN SPIRIT IS THIS FIERY RUM, which is popular in Jamaica, Barbados, and other English-speaking islands. I like to use a dark rum, such as Myers's or Appleton.

½ to 1 cup bird peppers or Scotch bonnets
10 allspice berries
2 whole cloves

1 sprig of thyme
1 bottle dark rum

Prepare as you would the sherry peppers, using rum in place of sherry.

Volcanic Hot Sauce

Ten years ago, few people outside the Caribbean had even heard of Scotch bonnet chilies. Today we can't seem to live without them! To call this lantern-shaped chili hot would be an understatement: the Scotch bonnet is fifty times more fiery than a jalapeño. But behind the heat there's a floral, almost fruity flavor that makes people think of apricots.

Mexico's habanero, Jamaica's country pepper, and Florida's datil pepper make satisfactory substitutes for Scotch bonnets. You could also use a milder chili, like the serrano or jalapeño, but the flavor won't be the same. If a milder, but still plenty fiery sauce is desired, seed and devein the Scotch bonnets.

The Scotch bonnet lends firepower to hot sauces throughout the Caribbean. A hellish condiment based on this hot sauce is featured at the stunning Cap Juluca resort in Anguilla. The chef will serve the blistering sauce straight to any guest bold enough to ask it. More often, he adds a few drops to other sauces to enliven his unique fusion of island and French cuisine.

Warning: This will probably be the hottest hot sauce you have ever tasted. A little goes a *long* way. But you'll surely grow to love it.

10 to 12 Scotch bonnets, stemmed (see Note)	2 tablespoons olive oil
6 garlic cloves, peeled and coarsely chopped	1 teaspoon molasses
⅓ cup fresh lime juice	½ teaspoon turmeric
⅓ cup distilled white vinegar	1 tablespoon salt, or to taste
2 tablespoons Dijon-style mustard	

Combine the pepper, garlic, lime juice, vinegar, mustard, oil, molasses, turmeric, and salt in a blender and puree until smooth. Correct the seasoning, adding more salt or molasses to taste.

Transfer the sauce to a clean bottle. You can use it right away, but the flavor will improve if you let it age for a few days. Volcanic Hot Sauce will keep almost indefinitely, refrigerated or at room temperature. Just give it a good shake before using.

Makes 2 cups.

NOTE: For information about handling Scotch bonnets, see page 32.

This is the simplest of all Caribbean hot sauces, the requisite accompaniment to such French West Indian stews as *blaff de poisson* and court-bouillon. You even find it as far north as Key West, where it goes by the name of old sour.

Spoon Chili Lime Sauce over grilled vegetables, chicken, or seafood. Add a few drops to perk up soups and stews. It's also great in salad dressings.

1 to 3 Scotch bonnets or other hot chilis
1 cup fresh lime juice (about 6 limes)
1 tablespoon salt

Stem, wash, seed, and thinly slice the peppers. (For a hotter sauce, leave the seeds in.) Combine the lime juice and salt in a mixing bowl and whisk until the latter is completely dissolved. Stir in the peppers.

Transfer the sauce to a clean jar or bottle. Let the mixture "ripen" at room temperature for at least 24 hours, preferably 5 days to a week.

Chili Lime Sauce will keep for several months at room temperature and it just improves with age.

Makes 1 cup.

Pika (Dutch West Indian Pickled Onion Sauce)

Visit the old market in willemstad, Curaçao, and you'll witness a scene right out of a plantation-house kitchen. Legions of cooks (some in plastic garbage-bag aprons) toil over battered, blackened pots bubbling away over charcoal fires. The fare is simple and elemental: fried fish with *funchi* (cornmeal mush), *stoba* (goat or conch stew), *tutu* (black-eyed pea and cornmeal mash). It's served without ceremony at vast communal tables under a corrugated tin roof. It's cheap. It's filling. And it's a perfect reminder of the roots of Caribbean cooking.

Whatever you order, you'll receive a jar of pika, the ubiquitous Dutch Antilles hot sauce. The tartness of this condiment is perfect for cutting the richness of the traditional stews and cornmeal dishes. Spoon it over steaks and other grilled fare. We're not talking the tongue-torturing chili sauces of Trinidad or the French islands, although some pikas can be quite hot. Of course, masochists can increase the number of Scotch bonnets (see page 32).

1 large red onion, finely chopped
  (about 1½ cups)
1 Scotch bonnet pepper, seeded and thinly
  sliced (for a hotter sauce leave the seeds in)

1½ cups distilled white vinegar
4 teaspoons salt

Combine the onion, pepper, vinegar, and salt in a large jar with a tight-fitting lid and shake until the salt is dissolved. Let the sauce "ripen" for at least 24 hours before serving, preferably for 2 to 3 days.

Pika will keep for several months at room temperature.

Makes 2 cups.

Tʜɪs sᴀꜰꜰʀᴏɴ-ᴄᴏʟᴏʀᴇᴅ ᴏɪʟ is used throughout the Spanish Caribbean to give an inviting orange hue to soups, stews, and rice dishes. Cuba's *arroz con pollo* and Puerto Rico's *asopao* would look positively anemic without it.

But that's only a start. I like to drizzle this brightly colored oil over carpaccio (especially fish carpaccio), grilled and steamed vegetables, and salads. Mix it with garlic and mayonnaise to make a Caribbean aioli.

I've taken some liberties with the traditional recipe, adding peppercorns, garlic, and chili peppers. If you prefer a conventional oil, leave these ingredients out.

2 cups olive oil

¼ cup annatto seeds (see Note)

8 garlic cloves (optional)

20 black peppercorns (optional)

1 Scotch bonnet or 2 jalapeño chili peppers, cut into quarters and seeded (optional; see page 32)

Heat the oil in a heavy saucepan over medium heat.

Add the annatto seeds, garlic, peppercorns, and peppers and cook until the oil is reddish gold and the annatto seeds begin to crackle, 3 to 5 minutes. Do not overcook, or the oil will become bitter. Remove the pan from the heat and strain the oil into a heatproof bowl to cool.

Transfer the oil to a clean glass bottle, using a funnel or measuring cup with a sharp spout. Store Annatto Oil away from heat and light. You don't need to refrigerate it. It will keep for several months, but the sooner you use it, the fresher it will taste.

Makes 2 cups.

ɴᴏᴛᴇ: Annatto is a rust-colored seed native to the Caribbean. Other names include achiote and roucou. Look for it at Hispanic and West Indian markets and most supermarkets, especially ones with a large Hispanic clientele. Annatto has a mild, earthy flavor with an iodine tang that reminds some people of oysters.

ᴠᴀʀɪᴀᴛɪᴏɴ: To make Annatto Butter, prepare the preceding recipe using clarified butter instead of olive oil.

Mango Vinegar

Is THERE ANY FLAVOR MORE EVOCATIVE of the tropics than mango? This kidney-shaped fruit possesses a succulent orange flesh with an intense peach-pineapple flavor and a spicy aftertaste that leans to turpentine in some varieties. It is, in short, the quintessence of a tropical fruit.

Mango Vinegar isn't a traditional West Indian ingredient, but it certainly fits within the Caribbean palate. Use it to give a tropical accent to vinaigrettes, chutneys, and pickles. A few drops of mango vinegar are just the thing for perking up soups, stews, and sauces.

Instructions on buying and ripening mangoes are found on page 108.

1 (24-ounce) bottle rice vinegar, white wine vinegar, or distilled white vinegar

1 small ripe mango

1 Scotch bonnet pepper, quartered and seeded

Pour 1 cup vinegar into a measuring cup. Peel the mango and cut the flesh off the seed in long, thin strips. Place the mango strips and chili pepper in the vinegar bottle and refill the bottle with vinegar.

Let the vinegar steep for at least 1 week before using.

Mango Vinegar will keep for several months, provided the mango pieces remain submerged. Store in a cool, dark place: it will keep almost indefinitely.

Makes 3 cups.

THIS ARDENT OIL turns up in various incarnations throughout the islands. Its ancestor may be piri-piri, a fiery olive oil–based condiment brought to the West Indies by indentured laborers from Madeira. The Portuguese came to Guyana, Grenada, and Trinidad in the mid-nineteenth century to replace the newly emancipated slaves in the cane fields. This particular recipe was inspired by our friend Eddy Stakelborough, owner of Eddy's Restaurant and Eddy's Ghetto in St. Barthélemy.

Pimiento (*bois d'inde* in French) is the leaf of the allspice tree, an aromatic seasoning similar to bay leaf, but with a sweet, perfumed flavor. You may be able to find it at a West Indian market. If not, substitute a bay leaf and a few allspice berries.

Drizzle Fire Oil over pizzas, salads, soups, grilled fish, and roast chicken. Packaged in an attractive bottle, it makes a heartwarming present. (The heart isn't all that it warms!)

Caribbean chilies are discussed at length on page 10. As in other recipes, I give a range for these fiery chilies. One chili will give you baby hot oil; four chilies will send you diving for your beer.

1 to 4 Scotch bonnets or other hot chilies

4 garlic cloves

20 black peppercorns

5 allspice berries

3 sprigs of fresh thyme

2 allspice leaves or bay leaves

3 to 4 cups extra-virgin olive oil

Stem and wash the chilies. Cut the large ones lengthwise into quarters, the small ones in half. For hotter oil, leave the seeds intact; for milder oil, remove them. For a very mild oil, leave the chilies whole.

Place the chilies, garlic, peppercorns, allspice, thyme, and leaves in a clean, decorative bottle. Top off the bottle with oil. Let the oil steep for at least 2 weeks before serving.

Fire Oil will keep for several months at room temperature. Store it away from heat and light.

Makes 3 to 4 cups.

Caribbean Carpaccio

CARPACCIO IS AN ITALIAN DISH, of course, but West Indians have a longstanding tradition of serving uncooked marinated seafood. Consider Cuba's escabeche (pickled shark), for example, or the conch salad of the Bahamas.

Although the fish in this recipe isn't exposed to heat, it isn't completely raw. The acidity in the lime juice "cooks" it. For a Hispanic accent you could use the Annatto Oil on page 61 instead of the chili oil called for below.

The type of fish you use is less important than its freshness. Feel free to substitute the freshest available fish in your area for any of the species mentioned below. For that matter, a beef or veal carpaccio could be prepared the same way.

OPPOSITE
*Caribbean Carpaccio
with Annatto Oil
(page 61)*

8 ounces very fresh grouper, snapper, tuna, or salmon

2 to 3 tablespoons fresh lime juice, plus 4 lime wedges for garnish

1 to 2 tablespoons Fire Oil (page 63)

Salt and freshly ground black pepper

1 shallot, minced

2 tablespoons minced fresh chives

2 tablespoons minced fresh flat-leaf parsley

2 tablespoons minced fresh cilantro, tarragon, or other herb

Slice the fish on the diagonal as thin as possible. Place the slices between 2 sheets of plastic wrap and gently flatten with the side of a meat cleaver to obtain paper-thin slices. Use these slices to carpet 4 dinner plates. (The easiest way to transfer the fish is to peel off one sheet of plastic wrap, invert the fish onto the plate, and peel off the second sheet of plastic wrap.)

Drizzle the lime juice and oil over the fish and season with salt and pepper. Sprinkle the minced shallots and fresh herbs on top. Gently pat the fish with your fingertips to work in the flavorings. Garnish each plate with lime wedges and serve at once.

Serves 4.

Enchilado Sauce

To most americans, *enchilado* suggests a dish made with tortillas. In Cuba and the Dominican Republic, the term refers to a soulful stew of garlic, peppers, and seafood (usually lobster or shrimp). The ingredients vary from region to region and cook to cook; white wine would be used in Havana and western Cuba, for example, beer in the east Cuban province of Oriente.

While generally served with seafood, Enchilado Sauce is delicious over chicken or pasta. I like to think of it as Caribbean marinara sauce.

2 tablespoons olive oil
5 garlic cloves, minced
1 medium onion, finely chopped
$\frac{1}{2}$ red bell pepper, seeded and diced
$\frac{1}{2}$ green bell pepper, seeded and diced
1 teaspoon dried oregano
$\frac{3}{4}$ teaspoon ground cumin, or to taste
1 bay leaf

$\frac{1}{2}$ cup tomato paste
Approximately $1\frac{1}{2}$ cups beer, or 1 cup
   dry white wine
1 tablespoon red wine vinegar
$\frac{1}{4}$ cup finely chopped fresh cilantro or
   flat-leaf parsley
Salt and freshly ground black pepper

Heat the olive oil in a large sauté pan or saucepan. Add the garlic, onion, bell peppers, oregano, cumin, and bay leaf and cook, stirring often, over medium heat until just beginning to brown, about 4 minutes.

Stir in the tomato paste, beer, vinegar, half the cilantro, and the salt and pepper. Bring the sauce to a boil, stirring well. Reduce the heat and gently simmer the sauce until well flavored, about 10 minutes. Stir in the remaining cilantro and correct the seasoning, adding salt or a few drops more of vinegar to taste.

To make Seafood Enchilado, combine the sauce with 1½ pounds shrimp, diced lobster, or fish. Simmer the seafood in the sauce until just firm, about 2 minutes.

To save the sauce for later use, transfer it to sterile jars with tight-fitting lids. Refrigerated, the sauce will keep for 1 week.

Makes 2 cups.

NOTE: Some Cuban cooks would use cachucha peppers (also known as *aji dulce* or rocotillo peppers in Puerto Rico) instead of bell peppers. These tiny, pattypan squash–shaped peppers taste similar to bell peppers, but have a hint of the floral aroma of a Scotch bonnet. (Rest assured: they're not in the least hot.) If you live in an area with a large Hispanic community, you may be able to find cachucha peppers. In this recipe, you would use 10 to 12 cachuchas in place of the bell peppers.

Puerto Rican Mojito

OPPOSITE, FROM
LEFT TO RIGHT
Green Sofrito (page 55),
Ajilimojili (page 47),
Red Sofrito (page 54),
and Puerto Rican Mojito

LIVING IN MIAMI, I THINK OF MOJITO (pronounced mo-HE-to) as a Cuban mint julep. This refreshing blend of rum, sugar, lime juice, fresh mint, and club soda is Cuba's national cocktail. But the term has a very different meaning in Puerto Rico, where it refers to a tangy salsa made from tomatoes, capers, and cilantro.

Puerto Rican Mojito is traditionally served as a dipping sauce for plantain chips and *tostones* (fried mashed green plantains). It's also great for dipping tortilla chips and it makes an uncommon cocktail sauce for shrimp and other seafood.

This recipe has been adapted from the authoritative book *La Cocina Puertorriqueña de Hoy* ("Contemporary Puerto Rican Cuisine") by my friend Giovanna Huyke. *Aji dulce* (cachucha pepper) is described on page 67.

6 *aji dulce* peppers, or 1½ tablespoons diced
   red bell pepper
½ green bell pepper, diced
5 garlic cloves, coarsely chopped
2 shallots, coarsely chopped
1 ripe tomato, peeled and seeded
1½ tablespoons capers, drained
1½ teaspoons dried oregano

½ cup washed and stemmed
   cilantro leaves
¼ cup tomato paste
2 tablespoons extra-virgin olive oil
1 tablespoon lime juice
Salt and freshly ground black pepper
   to taste

Combine the peppers, garlic, shallots, tomato, capers, oregano and cilantro in a food processor and grind to a smooth puree. Work in the tomato paste, olive oil, lime juice, and salt and pepper.

Transfer the sauce to a clean jar with a nonreactive lid. Refrigerated, it will keep for 1 week.

Makes 2 cups.

JAMS, JELLIES, CHUTNEYS, PICKLES, AND PRESERVED FRUITS

Sweet Potato Jam

OPPOSITE
*Orange Pepper
Jelly (page 77),
Banana Jam (page 76),
and Sweet Potato Jam*

I FIRST HEARD ABOUT THIS JAM from a Guadaloupean friend. It sounded downright bizarre, but I love Caribbean sweet potatoes so much I couldn't resist trying it. I've since learned of other West Indian sweet potato confections, including a jamlike dessert popular in Cuba called *boniatillo*.

Caribbean sweet potatoes are different from the orange sweet potato familiar to most North Americans. The skin is a patchy purple, the flesh is firm and white, and the flavor is akin to that of roasted chestnuts. This sweet potato isn't particularly sweet.

Look for Caribbean sweet potatoes at Hispanic and West Indian markets as well as most supermarkets, especially those with a large Hispanic clientele. Often they're sold by their Spanish name, *boniato*. An American-style sweet potato will work in a pinch, but cut back on the sugar.

Serve the jam on toast, scones, or crumpets.

1 lemon

4 whole cloves

1½ pounds Caribbean sweet potatoes (boniato)

2 cups sugar, or to taste

1 cinnamon stick, 3 inches long

½ vanilla bean, cut in half lengthwise

¼ teaspoon freshly grated nutmeg

Remove 4 strips of zest (the oil-rich outer rind) from the lemon with a vegetable peeler. Tie the lemon zest and cloves in a small piece of cheesecloth. (Or wrap them in a piece of foil and pierce all over with a fork.) Squeeze the lemon juice into a large saucepan and add 4 cups water. Peel the sweet potatoes and finely dice them into the lemon water. Add the sugar, lemon and clove packet, cinnamon stick, vanilla bean, and nutmeg.

Bring the mixture to a boil. Reduce the heat and gently simmer until thick and jamlike, about 30 minutes. Using a spoon, skim off any foam that may rise to the surface as the jam cooks. The potatoes should be soft enough to fall apart on their own, but if they don't, mash them with the back of a wooden spoon. Remove and discard the lemon zest and cloves. I like to leave the vanilla bean and cinnamon stick in the jam.

Transfer the jam to sterile jars (two 1-pint jars or four 1-cup jars), filling each to within ⅛ inch of the top (see page 13). Screw on the lids. Invert the jars for 10 minutes, then reinvert.

This jam is rather perishable, so it's best to store even the sealed jars in the refrigerator. Once opened, the jam should be served within 4 to 5 days.

Makes about 2 pints.

Tomato Jam

I FIRST TASTED THIS OFFBEAT JAM at the lovely François Plantation restaurant in St. Barthélemy, where it was served with smoked foie gras. Here is my version. Sweet, tart, and a little salty, it would make a wonderful accompaniment to smoked meats, grilled or roast chicken, and seafood. It's also pretty outrageous eaten straight from a spoon.

According to chef Christian Picard, either red or green tomatoes can be used for the jam; if you use red, choose tomatoes that are ripe but slightly firm.

2 pounds tomatoes (3 to 4 large tomatoes)
2 tablespoons kosher salt
Approximately 1½ cups sugar

Peel the tomatoes. Using the tip of a knife, cut a 1-inch X in the bottom of each tomato. Cut out the stem end. Plunge the tomatoes into a large pot of boiling water for 15 to 30 seconds, or until the skin starts to loosen. Transfer the tomatoes with a slotted spoon to a bowl of ice water or rinse with cold water to cool. Drain well. Pull the skins off the tomatoes. Cut each tomato in half widthwise and wring out the seeds. Cut the tomato halves into 1-inch pieces.

Toss the peeled, seeded tomatoes with the salt in a mixing bowl. Transfer the tomatoes to a strainer over a bowl in the refrigerator. Let the tomatoes drain for at least 6 hours, preferably overnight.

The next day, rinse the salt off the tomatoes and blot dry. Weigh the tomatoes on a kitchen scale and transfer them to a heavy saucepan. Add half the weight of the tomatoes in sugar. Bring the mixture to a boil. Reduce the heat to low and gently simmer mixture until thick and jamlike, stirring often, 40 to 60 minutes.

Transfer the jam to canning jars that have been sterilized following the instructions on page 13. Fill the jar to within ⅛ inch of the top. Screw on the lids. Invert the jars for 10 minutes, then reinvert. Let the jam cool to room temperature, then refrigerate until serving.

The tomato jam will keep almost indefinitely in the refrigerator.

Makes 1¼ cups.

Nothing goes to waste in the kitchen of my Cuban friend, Elida Proenza. The skins and seeds left over from making Guava Shells (page 78) become a perfumed guava jam.

Guavas are sold at Hispanic and Caribbean markets, specialty greengrocers, and at an increasing number of supermarkets. Most stores sell guavas in their green state (they will be firm and dark green). To ripen guavas, store them in a loosely sealed paper bag at room temperature. A ripe guava will be squeezably soft to the touch (but not mushy) and intensely fragrant. You should be able to smell it the moment you enter your house.

The skins, seeds, and pulp from 3 pounds ripe
   guavas (you should have about 1 pound—
   save the shells for the recipe on page 78)
¾ to 1 cup sugar

½ vanilla bean, cut in half lengthwise
½ cinnamon stick, 3 inches long
½ teaspoon grated lemon zest

Combine the guava skins, seeds, and pulp and 2½ cups water in a large, heavy saucepan and bring to a boil. Reduce the heat and briskly simmer the mixture for 10 minutes. Remove the pan from the heat and let it cool slightly.

Transfer the mixture to a blender and puree. Wipe out the saucepan. Pour the puree through a strainer back into the saucepan, pressing with a rubber spatula or the back of a wooden spoon to extract as much liquid as possible. You should have about 2¾ cups.

Stir in the sugar, vanilla bean, cinnamon stick, and lemon zest. Gently simmer the jam until thick and concentrated, 20 to 30 minutes, stirring often. Taste for sweetness, adding more sugar as desired. Remove the pan from the heat, remove cinnamon stick and vanilla bean, and let cool slightly.

Spoon the jam into two 8-ounce canning jars that have been sterilized following the instructions on page 13. Fill the jars to within ⅛ inch of the top. Screw on the lids. Invert the jars for 10 minutes, then reinvert. Let the jam cool to room temperature, then refrigerate until serving.

The jam will keep for several months at room temperature or in the refrigerator. Refrigerate once opened; it will keep for up to 2 weeks in the refrigerator.

Makes about 2 cups.

Banana Jam

To most north americans a banana is, well, a banana. West Indians have dozens of varieties to choose from, from tiny finger bananas no bigger than a digit to jumbo red bananas that are as big around as a cucumber. My favorite banana for this jam is the apple banana (see page 96), but any ripe banana will do.

5 ripe bananas

3 tablespoons fresh lime juice

²/₃ cup fresh orange juice or water

1¹/₂ cups sugar

¹/₂ vanilla bean, split in half lengthwise
and cut into thirds

¹/₈ teaspoon salt

1 tablespoon banana liqueur (optional)

Peel the bananas and thinly slice or mash with a fork. Place the bananas in a heavy saucepan with the lime juice, orange juice, sugar, vanilla bean, and salt, and bring to a boil. Reduce the heat and gently simmer the banana jam until thick, about 30 minutes, stirring often. Stir in the banana liqueur and remove the pan from the heat. Leave the vanilla bean in the jam—it's pretty.

Spoon the jam into three 6-ounce canning jars that have been sterilized following the instructions on page 13. Fill the jars to within ¹/₈ inch of the top. Screw on the lids. Invert the jars for 5 minutes, then reinvert. Let the jam cool to room temperature.

Store the jam in a cool, dark place. Refrigerate the jam once opened; it will keep for several weeks.

Makes 2¹/₄ cups.

Handsome scotch bonnet chili peppers, daintily dimpled and light red, green, orange, or yellow in hue, are an indispensable ingredient in West Indian cooking—and are becoming so in North American as well. Pepper jelly is a popular condiment in the American South and Southwest, of course, but few pack the firepower of this one.

2 red bell peppers

2 yellow bell peppers (or more red)

1 green bell pepper

2 to 4 Scotch bonnet chili peppers, or to taste
  (see Note)

2 tablespoons finely chopped fresh ginger

1 cup Mango Vinegar (page 62) or cider vinegar

¼ cup fresh orange juice

1 teaspoon freshly grated orange zest

1 (1¾-ounce) package dried fruit pectin
  (such as Sure-Jell)

1 teaspoon butter

5 cups sugar

Core and seed the bell peppers and Scotch bonnets. Finely chop the bell peppers and mince the hot peppers. You should have about 4 cups total.

Combine the peppers, ginger, vinegar, orange juice, orange zest, pectin, and butter in a large, nonreactive saucepan and bring to a rolling boil. Stir in the sugar and boil for 1 minute. With a metal spoon, skim off any foam that rises to the surface.

Sterilize six 1-cup canning jars following the instructions on page 13 and spoon the jelly into them. Fill the jars to within ⅛ inch of the top. Screw on the lids. Invert the jars for 10 minutes, then reinvert. Let the jelly cool to room temperature, shaking the jars periodically to distribute the peppers evenly.

Unopened, the jelly will keep for several months in the refrigerator or in a cool, dark place. Refrigerate once opened.

Makes 6 cups.

NOTE: For information on how to handle Scotch bonnets, see page 32.

Guava Shells

THE GUAVA IS ONE OF THE MOST ENTICING FRUITS of the tropics. A cousin of the clove and bay tree, it possesses a haunting musky aroma and a flavor reminiscent of honey, banana, and lemon. Guavas can be as small as an egg or as large as an orange, with a green, yellow, or white skin and a soft, moist flesh ranging from pale yellow to salmon in color.

There's only one drawback: the flesh is riddled with myriad hard, tiny black seeds. This makes eating fresh guava a frustrating and messy experience. For this reason, guavas are most often consumed in the form of jams, jellies, and nectar. Guava shells poached in sugar syrup (the shell is what's left of the fruit when you remove the skin and seeds) are a popular dessert in the Spanish Caribbean, where they are often served with salty cheese.

This and the Guava Jam recipe on page 75 are designed to take full advantage of guavas. The skins and seeds are transformed into guava jam; the shells are poached in syrup to make a dulcet dessert. Serve Guava Shells with finger-size pieces of *queso blanco* (a salty white cheese) or cream cheese. Guava shells are also great spooned over ice cream or whipped into milkshakes.

3 pounds ripe guavas (8 to 12 fruits)	2 to 2½ cups sugar
2 whole cloves	½ vanilla bean, cut in half lengthwise
2 strips lemon zest	½ cinnamon stick, 1½ inches long

Peel the guavas with a vegetable peeler or paring knife. Cut each in half lengthwise and scrape out the seeds with a melon baller or spoon. Save the skins and seeds for the jam on page 75. You should be left with ¼-inch-thick shells. Stick 1 clove in each strip of lemon zest.

Combine 3 cups of water, 2 cups sugar, the lemon strips, vanilla bean, and cinnamon stick in a heavy saucepan and bring to a boil. Reduce the heat to a simmer and add the guava shells. Gently simmer until very tender, 15 to 25 minutes. Taste the poaching liquid for sweetness, adding more sugar as desired. Skim the mixture from time to time to remove any foam or impurities that may rise to the surface.

Remove the pan from the heat and let cool slightly. Leave in the vanilla bean and cinnamon stick. Transfer the guava shells with their syrup to sterile jars (see page 13). Invert the jars for 10 minutes, then reinvert. Refrigerated, the shells will keep for several weeks.

Makes 16 to 24 shells, about 1 pint.

Most north americans consider the tomato a vegetable, using it chiefly for savory dishes. Botanically speaking, however, the tomato is a fruit. It is used as such in the Dominican Republic, where dulce de tomate—candied tomatoes—is a popular dessert.

This recipe was inspired by one from Julia Alvarez, alternate ambassador from the Dominican Republic to the United Nations and mother of an acclaimed novelist of the same name. She recommends serving it with cream cheese or *queso blanco* (a salty white cheese), much as you'd serve the Mango "Cheese" on page 108. Candied tomatoes also make an interesting addition to salads and can be served over ice cream or frozen yogurt.

The tomato of choice for this recipe is a ripe but still firm plum tomato.

1 pound plum tomatoes

1 cup sugar

½ cup raisins

1 cinnamon stick, 2 inches long

1 piece of vanilla bean, 2 inches long, split

Stem and wash the tomatoes and cut each in half lengthwise. Combine the sugar, 1 cup of water, the raisins, cinnamon stick, and vanilla bean in a heavy saucepan and bring to a boil.

Add the tomatoes, reduce the heat to medium, and gently simmer the tomatoes until soft but not mushy, about 10 minutes. Leave in the cinnamon stick and vanilla bean.

Transfer the tomatoes with their syrup to sterile jars (see page 13). Invert the jars for 10 minutes, then reinvert and let cool. Store in a cool, dark place. Refrigerate the tomatoes once opened.

Makes 1½ pints.

I FIRST TASTED THIS UNCOMMON PRESERVE at the *Fête des Cuisinières* (Festival of the Female Cooks) in Guadaloupe. Every summer, on the Day of St. Lawrence (a Christian martyr who, appropriately, was burned to death on a grill), women cooks from all over the island gather at St. Pierre Cathedral for a special mass, then parade through the streets of Point-à-Pitre dressed in madras gowns, bearing baskets of fruits and platters of food. They converge on a schoolyard for a huge block party and Creole feast.

During the apéritif hour, a jar of candied starfruit is passed from table to table. Guests are invited to place a slice of starfruit or two and a tablespoon of the syrup in their glasses, then add a shot of rum. The resulting beverage goes down with astonishing ease and loosens you up for the dancing of the *béguine* that follows. Candied starfruit also makes a great topping for ice cream or frozen yogurt.

Adjust the sugar in the following recipe according to the sweetness of the fruit.

OPPOSITE
*Candied Starfruit
and Banana Chutney
(page 96)*

3 pound starfruit (about 1¼ to 1½ starfruit; see Note)
2 cups sugar
½ vanilla bean, cut in half lengthwise

Wash the starfruit and trim off any green ends. Cut the fruits widthwise into ½-inch slices, removing any seeds with a fork.

Combine the sugar, 1 cup of water, and the vanilla bean in a large saucepan and bring to a boil. Stir in the starfruit and simmer, uncovered, until very tender, about 5 minutes. Taste for sweetness, adding sugar as necessary. (You probably won't need more unless you use very tart starfruit.) Leave in the vanilla bean.

Transfer the starfruit with its syrup to sterile jars (see page 13) and tightly cover. The starfruits will keep for several months in the refrigerator.

Makes 2 pints.

NOTE: Starfruit, also known as carambola, is a ridged yellow fruit that, when sliced widthwise, yields perfect five-pointed stars. To this decorative feature, add a crisp but succulent flesh and a refreshingly acidic flavor with hints of orange, grape, and lychee and you'll understand the fruit's appeal. When buying starfruit look for crisp, heavy fruits with firm, fat ribs. Avoid fruits that are bruised, limp, or oozing.

Candied Shaddock/Grapefruit Peel

Visit a west indian market and you may see something that looks like a giant, pear-shaped grapefruit. This is a shaddock (*chadec* in French), sometimes called a pumelo, the largest of all citrus fruits and the ancestor of the grapefruit. Native to Southeast Asia, the shaddock seems to have reached the Caribbean in the seventeenth century and is widely enjoyed today. Legend has it that the fruit is named for a Captain Shaddock, who is supposed to have brought it to Barbados.

Shaddock tastes like grapefruit, but the flesh is drier, so you can break it into segments, like an orange. Shaddock also has a thicker skin than grapefruit, which makes it ideal for candying. Candied shaddock rind is a popular snack throughout the Caribbean.

Shaddock is available on a limited basis at specialty greengrocers and West Indian and Asian markets. If unavailable, use thick-skinned grapefruits. The rinds of other citrus fruits can be candied the same way.

1 shaddock or 2 thick-skinned grapefruits	3 cups sugar
Salt	2 slices of ginger, ¼ inch thick
1 tablespoon baking soda	

Scrub the outside of the fruit well. Cut the fruit in half and remove the pulp (use for juice or salads). Scrape the inside rind clean, using a spoon or melon baller. Cut the rind into strips the size of your little finger.

Place the rinds in a large saucepan with cold salted water to cover. (You'll need about 1 tablespoon salt to every 3 cups water.) Boil the shaddock or grapefruit for 1 minute. Drain in a colander and rinse under cold water. Repeat this process 3 times to remove some of the bitterness from the rinds.

Place the rinds in a bowl with cold water to cover. Add the baking soda and let stand for 10 minutes. This removes more of the bitterness.

Combine 2 cups sugar, 1 cup water, and the ginger in a saucepan and bring to a boil without stirring. (I don't like to stir sugar when cooking. You can change the crystalline structure.) Add the shaddock, partly cover the pan, and gently simmer over medium-low heat until the rinds are soft and translucent and most of the syrup is absorbed, 30 to 40 minutes. Remove the pan from the heat and let the shaddock strips cool completely in the syrup.

Transfer the strips to a cake rack over a baking sheet to drain. Leave the shaddock until dry, 12 to 24 hours.

Place the remaining sugar in a shallow bowl. Dredge the shaddock pieces in sugar, shaking off the excess, and transfer them to an airtight box, with sheets of waxed paper between layers. Store in a cool, dark place. The candied rind will keep for several months.

Makes 60 to 70 pieces.

Caribbean Rumtopf

Rumtopf is the german term for a large glass jar of fresh fruits preserved in spirits. A similar preparation can be found throughout the French West Indies, where bartenders build magnificent fruit punches by steeping pineapples, starfruit, guavas, and other tropical fruits in rum and spices in huge glass demijohns. The fruit acquires a heady rum flavor, while the rum is transformed into punch. Use the following recipe as a guide, varying the fruits according to seasonal availability.

2 oranges

½ pineapple

2 ripe papayas (about 24 ounces)

6 apple bananas (see page 96) or
   regular bananas

1 tablespoon fresh lime juice

2 ripe mangoes (about 2 pounds)

4 ripe guavas

3 atemoyas, cherimoyas, or soursops
   (optional; see Note)

2 to 3 starfruit

2 to 3 cups raw (turbinado) sugar or
   granulated sugar (see Note)

2 vanilla beans, cut in half lengthwise,
   then in half crosswise

4 cinnamon sticks, 3 inches long,
   broken in half

6 cups light or dark rum, or
   as needed

Cut the oranges into ¼-inch slices. Peel and core the pineapple and cut widthwise into ¼-inch slices. Peel and seed the papayas and cut into ½-inch slices. Peel and cut the bananas into ½-inch slices and sprinkle with lime juice to prevent discoloring. Peel the mangoes and cut the flesh off the seeds. Cut the guavas, atemoyas, and starfruits crosswise into ½ inch slices.

(continued)

Rinse a large (at least 1-gallon) jar with boiling water. Layer the orange slices on the bottom. Sprinkle the oranges with ⅓ to ½ cup sugar and place a piece of vanilla bean and cinnamon stick on top. Add a layer of pineapple and sprinkle with more sugar, vanilla, and cinnamon. Continue layering the fruits in this fashion until all are used up.

Pour enough rum over the fruit to submerge it by 2 inches. Tightly seal the jar. Let the fruits steep in a cool, dark place for at least 3 weeks or as long as 3 months. The longer the fruit steeps, the tastier it will be.

Rumtopf can be served two ways. Ladle the rum into glasses for sipping straight or over ice. (As the rum level goes down, you can add more; keep the fruits submerged.) Serve the fruit in bowls by itself or over ice cream.

Makes 1 gallon.

NOTE: Atemoya, cherimoya, and soursop are tropical fruits with a custardlike consistency and a sweet-tart, musky taste. The first looks like a swollen artichoke; the second is green and irregularly shaped; the third is covered with tiny Velcro-like barbs. Look for these fruits at specialty greengrocers, well-stocked supermarkets, and Hispanic and West Indian markets. All three will be squeezably soft when ripe.

You can use granulated sugar, but raw sugar has a little more flavor.

Fruit curds and fruit "cheeses" (see page 106) were in vogue in eighteenth- and nineteenth-century England. Their popularity was fueled by the growing supply and diminishing price of Caribbean sugar. The traditional fruit for curd is lemon, of course, but passion fruit gives the recipe an explosive tropical flavor.

Passion fruit is discussed at length on page 117. Depending on the size and juiciness of the fruit, you'll need 8 to 12 fruits to make ¾ cup juice. You can also use the frozen passion fruit juice sold at West Indian markets or supermarkets with a large Hispanic clientele. If you can't find fresh or frozen passion fruit, try the bottled juice available at some liquor stores, but add a couple of tablespoons of fresh lime juice to perk up the flavor.

Use this curd as a filling for fruit tarts and meringue pies. It's also delectable eaten straight from a spoon!

¾ cup passion fruit juice

¾ cup sugar

8 egg yolks or 4 whole eggs

½ cup (1 stick) unsalted butter,
cut into ½-inch pieces

Place the passion fruit juice, sugar, eggs, and butter in a heavy nonreactive saucepan and whisk to mix.

Place the pan over medium heat and, whisking steadily, cook the mixture until thick and smooth, 3 to 4 minutes. Do not let it boil or it will curdle.

Transfer the curd to a sterile jar (see page 13). Press a piece of plastic wrap over the surface of the curd to prevent a skin from forming while it cools. Make a few small slits in the plastic wrap with the tip of a sharp knife to allow the steam to escape. When the curd is cool, remove the plastic wrap and cover the jar.

Passion Fruit Curd will keep for several weeks in the refrigerator.

Makes 2 cups.

Hᴇʀᴇ's ᴀ ᴄᴀʀɪʙʙᴇᴀɴ ᴛᴡɪsᴛ on classic Florida key lime pie. The filling is the Passion Fruit Curd on page 87. There are two options for toppings: meringue and whipped cream. Both have their partisans, so I've included instructions for each.

For the crust:

1½ cups graham cracker crumbs (preferably cinnamon graham crackers)

½ cup melted butter

2 tablespoons sugar

2 cups Passion Fruit Curd (page 87)

For a whipped cream topping:

1 cup heavy cream

3 tablespoons confectioners' sugar, or to taste

1 teaspoon vanilla extract

For a meringue topping:

4 egg whites

½ teaspoon cream of tartar

⅔ cup sugar

½ teaspoon grated lemon or orange zest

whole nutmeg, for grating

Preheat the oven to 400°F. Combine the graham cracker crumbs, melted butter, and sugar in a mixing bowl and stir to mix. Use this mixture to line the bottom and sides of an 8-inch pie pan, pressing with the back of a spoon to make a compact crust. Bake the crust until lightly browned, 8 to 10 minutes. Transfer to a cake rack to cool.

When the crust has cooled, spoon in the curd, smoothing the top with a wet spoon.

If using the meringue topping, preheat the oven to 450°F. In a mixer beat the egg whites and cream of tartar to soft peaks, starting at slow speed, gradually increasing to medium, then high. Add the sugar and continue beating until the whites are firm and shiny but not dry. Transfer the meringue to a piping bag fitted with a large star tip. Pipe rosettes of meringue all over the top of the pie.

Bake the pie until the top is nicely browned, 2 to 4 minutes. Do not leave the kitchen while the pie bakes; meringue burns easily. Let the pie cool to room temperature before serving. You can prepare the pie up to 4 hours ahead of time, but refrigerate it if you plan to wait more than 1 hour. Let it come to room temperature before serving.

If using the whipped cream topping, beat the cream to soft peaks in a bowl over ice (or freeze the bowl before beating). Sift in the confectioners' sugar and add the vanilla and lemon zest. Continue beating the cream to firm peaks. Do not overbeat. Transfer the whipped cream to a piping bag fitted with a large star tip. Pipe rosettes of cream all over the top of the pie. Grate a little fresh nutmeg on top. This version can also be prepared ahead, but pipe the whipped cream on the pie not more than 1 hour before serving.

Serves 8.

Nicaraguan Chile Criollo

H ERE'S A TANGY RELISH from the western corner of the Caribbean. Nicaraguans serve *chile criollo* (pronounced CHEE-lay-cree-YO-yo) with everything from grilled meats to fried fish to tortillas. One finds a similar relish throughout Central America and even in Haiti.

We've left the fiery realm of the Scotch bonnet. Nicaraguans prefer the gentler heat of a jalapeño pepper. But you could always spice things up with a hotter chili.

1 1/3 cups distilled white vinegar

1 tablespoon salt

1 teaspoon sugar

Freshly ground black pepper to taste

2 carrots, very finely chopped (about 1 cup)

1 large onion, very finely chopped
  (about 1 1/2 cups)

1 cup very finely chopped green cabbage

1 to 2 jalapeño peppers, very finely
  chopped, with the seeds (for a milder
  relish, remove the seeds)

2 tablespoon finely chopped fresh cilantro
  or flat-leaf parsley

Combine the vinegar, salt, sugar, and pepper in a mixing bowl and whisk until the sugar and salt are dissolved. Stir in the carrots, onion, cabbage, chilies, and cilantro. Correct the seasoning, adding salt, sugar, or vinegar to taste. The mixture should be highly seasoned.

Transfer the mixture to sterile jars (see page 13). Let the Chile Criollo stand at room temperature for at least 24 hours to cure. It will keep for several months in the refrigerator or in a cool, dark cupboard.

Makes about 3 cups.

I FIRST TASTED PICKLED LIMES at a roadside shack in Trinidad, where they were sold to passersby as a snack. Not long after, I came across a recipe for pickled limes in an old cookery manuscript, reprinted as *A Collection of 19th Century Jamaican Cookery and Herbal Recipes* by John Kenneth McKenzie Pringle (Mill Press, Kingston, Jamaica, 1990). What follows is a synthesis of several preparations.

Pickled limes are traditionally eaten as a snack or an accompaniment to "shark and bake" (Trinidadian fried shark sandwiches). Finely chopped, they make an intriguing addition to salads. (A small spoonful of pickled lime juice greatly invigorates a salad dressing.) Their zesty flavor goes well in any dish that needs a little excitement.

2 large limes

¼ cup kosher salt

1 Scotch bonnet pepper, cut in half and
  seeded (see page 32)

1 garlic clove

10 black peppercorns

3 whole cloves

3 allspice berries

Scrub the limes and dry well. Cut each lime into 8 wedges and cut each wedge in half. Remove any seeds. Place the limes in a bowl with the salt and mix well. Transfer the lime mixture to a sterile glass jar (see page 13). Add the chili pepper, garlic, peppercorns, cloves, and allspice and fill the jar with vinegar.

Place a piece of plastic wrap over the jar, affix the lid, and let the limes pickle at room temperature for at least 5 days, shaking the jar from time to time to mix the juices. This makes a very tasty but very strong lime pickle.

For a milder pickle, drain the limes in a colander and rinse with cold water. Return the limes to the jar and add cold water to cover. Let stand for 2 days.

Store the Pickled Limes in a cool, dark place or in the refrigerator, where they will keep for several months.

Makes 1 cup.

Caribbean-Style Pickled Peppers

"Peter piper picked a peck of pickled peppers" runs the old tongue-twister. Not a peck of these, I'll wager! The Scotch bonnet pepper and its cousins, the Mexican habanero and French West Indian piment, are the world's hottest peppers—fifty times hotter than the once-feared jalapeño. Red, yellow, orange, or green, this walnut-size flamethrower has a dimpled crown that makes it look like a Chinese lantern or, with a little imagination, a Highlander's bonnet.

Scotch bonnets are becoming increasingly available at gourmet shops, supermarkets, and, of course, West Indian markets. For information on how to handle them, see page 32. If unavailable, you could use one of the aforementioned chilies or, if you live in Florida, datil peppers. Any chili can be pickled in this fashion, but the flavor won't be the same.

Warning: These peppers are exceedingly hot. The sadist will delight in giving them as a gift; the masochist will gobble them with gusto.

20 Scotch bonnet peppers

2 medium onions

2 carrots

3 cups distilled white vinegar

1 tablespoon salt

2 teaspoons sugar

10 allspice berries

Stem and wash the peppers and blot dry with paper towels. Cut any large chilies in half; leave the smaller ones whole. Peel the onions and carrots and cut into ¼-inch slices.

Combine the vinegar, 1 cup water, the salt, and sugar in a bowl and whisk until the sugar and salt are dissolved. Add the allspice.

Layer the chilies, onions, and carrots in glass jars you've previously washed inside and out with boiling water (see page 13). Add enough vinegar mixture to immerse the chilies completely. Cover the jars with nonreactive lids.

Let the peppers pickle at room temperature for at least 3 days or as long as 1 week before serving. Serve the peppers, onions, and carrots the way you would pickles or relishes. The pickling liquid makes a tasty hot sauce.

Pickled peppers will keep for several months at room temperature. Refrigerate after opening.

Makes two 1-pint jars.

Green Mango Chutney

To most north americans, mango means ripe mango, a luscious fruit that's aptly been called the peach of the tropics. But for centuries, Caribbean cooks have used green (unripe) mangoes as a vegetable, salad ingredient, and base for a broad range of table sauces.

In the French islands, for example, you find a spicy green mango relish called *rougail de mangue verte*, while in Trinidad and Tobago pickled green mangoes are a popular snack. Most of the English islands have some sort of green mango chutney.

Green Mango Chutney makes a great accompaniment to poultry, ham, and roast pork. You can also make the chutney with ripe mangoes, but you'll need to shorten the cooking time to 15 minutes and cut back on the sugar.

2 pounds green or semiripe mangoes
  (2 to 3 large mangoes)
1 cinnamon stick, 3 inches long
5 black peppercorns
5 whole cloves
2 cardamom pods
1 medium red onion, finely chopped (about 1 cup)
1 red bell pepper, cored, seeded, and finely
  chopped (about 1 cup)
1/2 to 1 Scotch bonnet pepper, seeded and minced
  (for a hotter chutney leave the seeds in)
1 tablespoon minced fresh ginger

2 garlic cloves, minced
1 cup dried currants or raisins
Juice and grated zest of 1 orange (about
  1/2 cup juice, 1/2 teaspoon zest)
2/3 cup Mango Vinegar (page 62) or cider
  vinegar
1 1/4 to 1 1/2 cups brown sugar,
  or to taste
1/2 cup white rum
3/4 teaspoon salt (optional)
2 tablespoons minced fresh cilantro

Peel the mangoes. Tie the cinnamon stick, peppercorns, cloves, and cardamom in cheesecloth or wrap them in foil and perforate the resulting bundle with a fork.

Combine the mangoes, spice bundle, onion, bell pepper, Scotch bonnet, ginger, garlic, currants, orange juice and zest, vinegar, brown sugar, rum, and salt in a large, heavy saucepan and cook over medium heat, loosely covered, until the mango is soft but not mushy and the mixture is thick and richly flavored, about 30 minutes. Stir in the cilantro the last 2 minutes. Discard the spice bundle.

Taste the chutney for seasoning, adding more sugar or vinegar as necessary or even a splash of rum. The chutney should be a little sweet and a little sour.

Transfer the chutney to sterile jars (two 1-pint jars or four 1-cup jars), filling each to within ⅛ inch of the top (see page 13). Tightly seal the jars with covered lids. Invert the jars for 10 minutes, then reinvert.

Unopened, the chutney will keep for several months at room temperature. Refrigerate once opened; the chutney will keep for several weeks.

Makes about 2 pints.

NOTE: Some people are allergic to mango sap, a few drops of which may be found on the skin. You may wish to wear gloves when handling mango if you have sensitive skin.

Banana Chutney

CHUTNEY IS A SPICY FRUIT CONDIMENT traditionally served with curries. Like many Caribbean sauces, it originated in India (the Hindi name is *chatni*), where it was often made with mangoes. Today, virtually any fruit is fair game for the chutney pot and the tangy condiment is served with everything from crostini to roast meats. Baked ham, grilled chicken, and turkey sandwiches are immeasurably enhanced by its presence.

My favorite banana for the following chutney is the apple banana, a short, stubby fruit with a wonderful applelike aftertaste. Known as *plátano manzano* in Spanish and *pomme figue* in French, the apple banana is available in Hispanic markets and an increasing number of gourmet shops and supermarkets. But regular bananas will produce a tasty chutney, too.

5 ripe apple bananas or regular bananas

½ cup Tamarind Water (page 118)
  or balsamic vinegar

⅓ cup fresh lime juice

½ teaspoon grated lime zest

2 tablespoons minced candied ginger

½ to 1 Scotch bonnet pepper, seeded and
  minced (for a hotter chutney leave the seeds in)

1 red bell pepper, cored, seeded, and diced

1 green bell pepper, cored, seeded, and
  diced

⅔ cup brown sugar, or to taste

½ cup raisins

1 teaspoon ground coriander

½ teaspoon salt

Freshly ground black pepper to taste

Peel the bananas and cut into ½-inch slices. Place them in a large saucepan with the tamarind water, lime juice and zest, ginger, Scotch bonnets, bell peppers, brown sugar, raisins, coriander, salt, and pepper, and bring to a boil.

Reduce the heat and gently simmer until the bananas and peppers are soft but not mushy, about 10 minutes, stirring occasionally. Correct the seasoning, adding more lime juice or sugar to taste. The chutney should be a little sweet, a little sour, and quite spicy.

Transfer the chutney to sterile jars (two 1-pint jars or four 1-cup jars), filling each to within ⅛ inch of the top (see page 13). Screw the lids on the jars. Invert the jars for 10 minutes, then reinvert.

Unopened, the chutney will keep for several months at room temperature. Refrigerate once opened; the chutney will keep for several weeks.

Makes about 2 pints.

MANGOES (INDEED ANY FRUIT) may seem like an odd ingredient for ketchup. But in the eighteenth century, ketchups were made from walnuts, gooseberries, elderberries, currants, grapes—in short, just about everything but tomatoes. Tomato ketchup didn't really become popular until the mid-nineteenth century.

Mangoes have been used to make savory table sauces in the Caribbean for centuries. Mango chutney adorned the tables of English plantation owners. Mango pickles remain a popular snack in Trinidad and Tobago. This recipe isn't associated with one particular island, but it's certainly Caribbean in spirit.

Mango Ketchup makes a great accompaniment to roast chicken, ham, duck, and pork. It also is a great way to use up bruised mangoes.

3 pounds ripe mangoes

1 tablespoon olive oil

1/2 cup finely chopped shallots (6 to 8 shallots)

2 garlic cloves, minced

1 tablespoon minced fresh ginger

1 to 2 Scotch bonnet chilies, seeded, or
  2 jalapeño chilies, seeded and finely chopped

2/3 cup dark rum

1/2 cup cider vinegar, or to taste

1/4 cup brown sugar, or to taste

1/4 cup tomato puree

3 tablespoons molasses

1 tablespoon fresh lime juice, or to taste

1 teaspoon ground allspice

1/2 teaspoon freshly grated nutmeg

1/2 teaspoon ground coriander

1/2 teaspoon ground cinnamon

1/4 teaspoon ground cloves

Salt and plenty of freshly ground black
  pepper

Peel the mangoes, cut the flesh off the flat seed, and dice. You should have about 3 cups.

Heat the oil in a heavy saucepan over medium heat. Sauté the shallots, garlic, and ginger until soft and translucent but not brown. Stir in the mango, ginger, chilies, rum, vinegar, brown sugar, tomato puree, molasses, lime juice, allspice, nutmeg, coriander, cinnamon, cloves, and black pepper. Add 1/2 cup water and bring the mixture to a boil.

Reduce the heat, cover the pan, and gently simmer the ketchup until well flavored and saucelike (the mango pieces should be falling apart), about 20 minutes, stirring as necessary. Puree the mixture in a blender.

Strain the ketchup back into the saucepan and simmer for 1 minute. Correct the seasoning, adding additional salt and pepper, lime juice, or sugar to taste; the ketchup should be a little sweet, a little sour, and quite spicy. If it is too thick, add a little rum or water.

Transfer the ketchup to a clean jar or bottle. Refrigerated, it will keep for several months.

Makes 3 cups.

SNACKS AND SWEETS

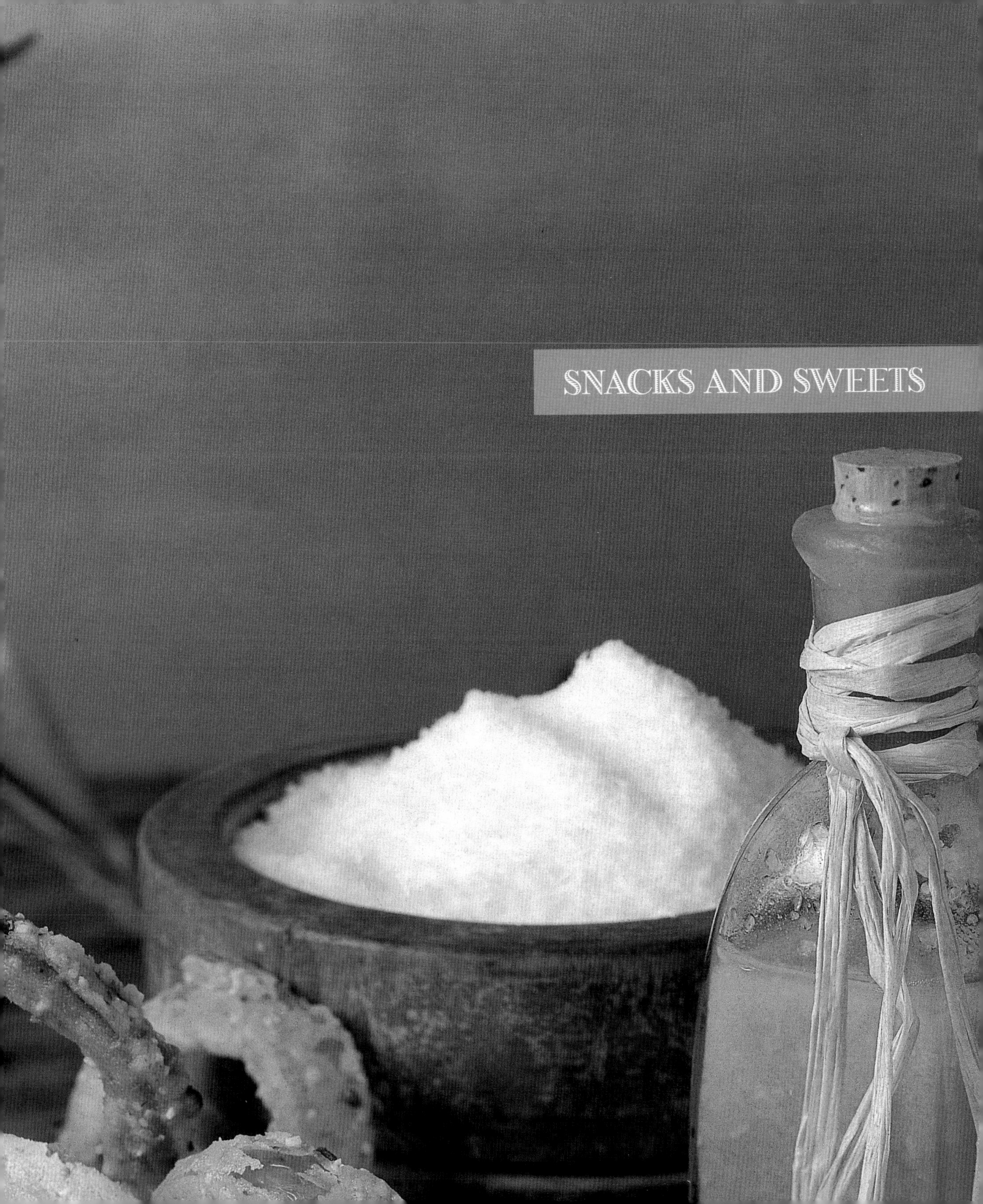

Spiced Channa

OPPOSITE
*Spiced Channa and
"Cooking in Paradise"
Planter's Punch
(page 130)*

CHANNA IS THE EAST INDIAN word for chickpea. Spiced roasted channa is a widely enjoyed snack in Trinidad, and its popularity has spilled over to other islands in the southern Caribbean. Spiced channa makes a great accompaniment to cocktails.

The spices are limited only by your imagination. The following recipe offers five possible seasonings based on recipes in this book.

A purist would probably use dried chickpeas. Soak them overnight in water to cover and boil them until tender, 1½ to 2 hours. You can also obtain perfectly tasty results with canned chickpeas.

4 cups cooked chickpeas, drained well
   and blotted dry
2 tablespoons extra-virgin olive oil

One of the following seasonings:

➤ 2 tablespoons Dry Jerk Seasoning (page 29
   or use a commercial brand)
or

➤ 2 tablespoons Cuban Adobo (page 26
   or use a commercial brand)
or

➤ 2 tablespoons Curry Powder (page 21
   or use a commercial brand)
   2 teaspoons salt
or

➤ 2 tablespoons Garam Masala (page 25
   or use a commercial brand)
   2 teaspoons salt
or

➤ 1 tablespoon cayenne pepper
   2 teaspoons ground cumin
   2 teaspoons ground black pepper
   2 teaspoons salt

Preheat the oven to 400°F.

In a large bowl toss the chickpeas with the oil and the seasoning mix of choice. Spread them in a single layer in a nonstick roasting pan and bake until the chickpeas are golden brown and crisp, 30 to 40 minutes.

Let the channa cool to room temperature, then store in an airtight box.

In theory the Spiced Channa will keep for several weeks, although at our house it's usually gone within a couple of hours. If the channa becomes soggy, you can crisp it by rebaking.

Makes about 2½ cups.

Tamarind Balls

I FIRST TASTED THIS TANGY SNACK at the Fruit and Spice Park in Homestead, Florida. I next tasted it at a roadside eatery on Trinidad's stunning north coast. The third time I enjoyed tamarind balls, I vowed, would be in my home, where I could be assured of a steady supply.

The addition of garlic and hot pepper to what is ostensibly a candy may seem odd to the North American palate, but the blurring of sweet and savory, of fruity and hot, is common throughout the sun belt.

Instructions on buying and peeling tamarind can be found on page 118.

1½ pounds fresh tamarind pods
  (about 2 cups peeled pulp)
1 garlic clove, minced
1 teaspoon salt

1 teaspoon freshly ground black pepper
½ teaspoon cayenne pepper
2 cups sugar, or as needed

Shell the tamarind pods and remove any strings from the pulp. Place the pulp in a mixing bowl. Add the garlic, salt, pepper, cayenne, and 1 cup sugar (or to taste). Knead together with your fingers to obtain a doughlike mixture.

Pinch off 1-inch pieces of the tamarind mixture and roll them into smooth balls between the palms of your hands. Place the remaining 1 cup sugar in a shallow bowl. Roll the tamarind balls in sugar until thoroughly coated, shaking off the excess.

Store the tamarind balls in an airtight container, leaving a little space between each ball. Place a sheet of waxed paper between layers. Stored in a cool, dry place, tamarind balls will keep for several months. Warn eaters to nibble around the seeds.

Makes about 40 tamarind balls.

CHIP-CHIPS BELONG to a beloved family of coconut-based confections that Trinidadians call sugar cakes. This version takes its name from the way the coconut is cut: in broad, thin, chiplike strips. A similar candy is made in the Bahamas, and indeed on most of the Caribbean islands. This recipe is inspired by one from Natalie's Shark and Bake Shop at Maracas Bay in northern Trinidad.

1 ripe (hard) coconut	1½ teaspoons ground cinnamon
1 pound dark brown sugar (about 3 cups)	¼ teaspoon ground cloves

Drain, crack, and shell the coconut as described on page 129. There's no need to peel off the brown skin. Cut the coconut into long, thin, curved strips no more than ⅛ inch thick. This is most easily done with a mandoline or a food processor, but can also be done by hand.

Place the brown sugar in a large, heavy saucepan and melt it over high heat, stirring with a wooden spoon. (Note: In this recipe you want to stir the sugar to make it soft and creamy.) Stir in the coconut, cinnamon, and cloves. Reduce the heat to medium-low and cook the mixture, stirring steadily, until it forms a thick mass that comes away from the sides of the pan, about 10 minutes.

Mound spoonfuls of the mixture on a lightly oiled baking sheet to form 2-inch circles, gently patting each with the back of the spoon to flatten it lightly. Let the Chip-Chips cool completely, then pry them off the baking sheet with a metal spatula.

Store the Chip-Chips in an airtight container away from heat and light. They'll keep for several weeks.

Makes about 24 Chip-Chips.

Coconut Chips

I FIRST ENCOUNTERED THESE CHIPS at a colorful restaurant in Barbados called Raffles. I can't think of a better accompaniment to a planter's punch or other rum drink.

When buying coconuts, look for ones that feel heavy in your hand. Shake the nut: you should be able to hear the liquid slosh around inside. A dry coconut is past its prime.

To open the coconut, punch out the eyes with a screwdriver and hammer. Invert the coconut over a glass and drain out the clearish liquid inside, the water. Coconut water makes a refreshing beverage in its own right (serve over ice) and is great mixed with rum and Falernum (page 122).

Wrap the drained coconut in a towel and smash it into five or six pieces with a hammer. (The towel prevents shards of the shell from flying.) Using a short, stiff-bladed knife, pry the coconut meat away from the shell. It's a good idea to wear heavy gloves when working with coconut to protect your hands. (To make the meat easier to remove from the shell, you can bake coconut pieces for about 20 minutes in a 400°F. oven. This will help loosen the meat from the shell.)

Trim the brown skin off the white meat with a paring knife. The coconut is now ready for slicing.

1 ripe (hard) coconut
Salt

Drain, open, shell, and peel the coconut as described above. Cut the coconut pieces into paper-thin chips, using a mandoline, vegetable peeler, or food processor fitted with a slicing blade. Preheat the oven to 350°F.

Arrange the strips on a baking sheet and lightly sprinkle with salt. Bake the chips until crisp and golden brown, 8 to 10 minutes, turning with a spatula to ensure even cooking. Transfer the chips to a wire rack to cool completely.

Store the chips in an airtight container away from heat or light. The chips will keep for up to a week, although they seldom survive the afternoon at our house. If they should become soft or soggy, you can rebake them until crisp.

Makes 2 to 3 cups.

Bolo Pretu (Dutch West Indian Fruitcake)

Say the words *bolo pretu* to a Dutch West Indian and his eyes will light with pleasure. This moist, dense fruitcake is the traditional wedding cake of the Dutch Antilles, and is also a popular dessert so generously steeped in brandy and other spirits that it will keep for half a year.

Bolo pretu literally means "black cake" in Papiamento, the musical Curaçaon dialect woven from Dutch, Spanish, Portuguese, and African languages. For weddings, the dark cake is traditionally garnished with a snow-white icing sprinkled with tiny silver candy balls (dragées). Guests get to enjoy the cake twice: first at the wedding, then as keepsake slices, which are fancifully wrapped to take home.

You can't really buy *bolo pretu* commercially, but every extended family seems to have someone who excels in its preparation. The following recipe was inspired by one from Carolina Amira, who works at the gorgeous new Sonesta Hotel near Willemstad.

Bolo Pretu is relatively simple to make, but you'll need at least two weeks from start to finish for steeping the ingredients in liquor and aging the finished cake. The orange liqueur of choice, naturally, is curaçao.

½ pound mixed candied fruits, including candied cherries, citron, orange peel, and lemon peel

½ pound mixed dried fruits, including raisins, currants, figs, pitted prunes, and dates

2 ounces pound cashew nuts

¼ cup curaçao (orange liqueur)

¼ cup crème de cacao or rum

¼ cup Malaga or marsala

¼ cup dark corn syrup

½ cup (1 stick) unsalted butter, at room temperature

¾ cup dark brown sugar

1 teaspoon burnt sugar (see Note; optional)

1 teaspoon ground cinnamon

½ teaspoon ground allspice

¼ teaspoon ground cloves

2 teaspoons vanilla extract

½ teaspoon almond extract

3 eggs

1 cup flour

Approximately 1 cup brandy or rum for basting

for the icing and garnish (optional):

6 tablespoons light corn syrup

¾ pound confectioners' sugar

2 tablespoons silver candy balls (dragées)

Coarsely grind the candied fruits, dried fruits, and cashews in a food processor or meat grinder. Transfer this mixture to a large bowl and stir in the curaçao, crème de cacao, Malaga, and dark corn syrup. Cover the bowl with plastic wrap and let this mixture steep in the refrigerator for at least 2 days or as long as 1 week.

Preheat the oven to 325°F. Cream the butter in an electric mixer. Add the brown sugar, burnt sugar, spices, and vanilla and almond extracts and beat until light and fluffy. Beat in the eggs one by one, scraping down the sides of the bowl with a rubber spatula after each. Add the fruit mixture with its soaking liquid, followed by the flour. Beat just to mix. Grease a 9-inch cake pan with butter or vegetable oil spray, line the bottom with parchment paper, and butter or oil again.

Spoon the batter into the pan and place in the oven. Bake the cake until set and an inserted toothpick comes out clean, about 1 hour. Transfer the cake pan to a rack and let cool to room temperature. Remove cake from pan. Technically, the *Bolu Pretu* can be eaten at this stage, but no Dutch Antillean would dream of doing so.

For the best results, sprinkle the cake with brandy or rum and tightly wrap in plastic. Transfer the cake to an airtight tin and store in a cool place or in the refrigerator. Every week or so, unwrap the cake and baste with more brandy. The cake will not only keep but continue to improve for several months.

If you'd like to ice the cake before serving, combine the light corn syrup and confectioners' sugar in a mixer and beat to a smooth white paste. Use this mixture to ice the cake. (If too thick, warm the icing over a pan of simmering water.) Sprinkle the cake with the silver balls and cut into squares or wedges for serving. Alternatively, the cake can be cut into pieces, wrapped in plastic, and decorated with ribbons for gift-giving.

Serves 10.

NOTE: Burnt sugar is a coloring and flavoring agent made from darkly caramelized sugar. This is what gives Bolo Pretu its characteristic black color. Burnt sugar is used throughout the Caribbean and can be found in West Indian markets. The cake is delicious without it, but it won't be as dark.

Mango "Cheese"

FRUIT "CHEESE" IS A POPULAR SWEET on the English Caribbean speaking islands. It's actually a sort of candy, a jellylike confection made by boiling down fresh fruit puree with sugar and sometimes gelatin. The guava paste (*pasta de guayaba*) enjoyed on the Spanish islands is nothing more than guava cheese.

The traditional way to serve fruit cheese is with a salty cheese, like *queso blanco*, gouda, cheddar, or even cream cheese. The saltiness of the dairy cheese helps counterbalance the sweetness of the fruit cheese. This combination of sweet and salty is particularly prized in the Spanish Caribbean and Latin America, where the pair are often served as a dessert.

When buying mangoes, look for unblemished fruits free of soft spots. Let them ripen at room temperature. When ripe, a mango will be squeezably soft and very fragrant. You can't go by color alone, as some varieties remain green even when ripe.

3 pounds ripe mangoes (3 to 4 mangoes)

3 tablespoons fresh lemon or lime juice

Approximately 3 cups sugar, plus 1 cup
   for dredging the cheese

3 envelopes unflavored gelatin

$\frac{1}{3}$ cup fresh orange juice or water

Peel the mangoes and cut the flesh off the seeds. Puree the flesh in a blender or food processor. Strain the mango puree into a measuring cup, pressing the pulp with the back of a spoon to extract as much juice as possible; you should have about 3 cups puree. Stir in the lemon juice.

Measure out an amount of sugar equal to the volume of the mango mixture. Sprinkle the gelatin over the orange juice in a small bowl and let stand until spongy, about 5 minutes.

Pour the mango mixture into a wide, heavy pan. Add the sugar and bring the mixture to a boil. Reduce the heat to medium and cook the mango mixture until very thick—it should come away from the sides of the pan—about 40 minutes, stirring often with a wooden spoon. Stir in the gelatin mixture and simmer for 2 minutes or until dissolved.

Pour the mixture into an 8-x-8-inch glass or ceramic baking dish you've lightly moistened with water. Place the dish on a cake rack and let cool until the mixture is set, 1 to 2 hours. Using a sharp knife, cut the "cheese" into 1-inch squares or diamonds. Pour the remaining 1 cup sugar into a shallow bowl. Dredge each piece of "cheese" in sugar and transfer to a tightly sealed box.

The cheese will keep for several months in a cool place.

Makes about sixty-five 1-inch pieces.

Jamaican Gingerbread

JAMAICA IS ONE OF THE WORLD'S LARGEST producers of ginger. So it should come as no surprise that ginger beer, ginger cookies, candied ginger, and gingerbread figure prominently in the island's culinary landscape.

Although gingerbread is an ancient dish (recipes for it can be found in medieval European cookbooks), it reached its apotheosis in the West Indies. After all, most of its ingredients are produced in the islands, from ginger, nutmeg, and allspice to molasses, brown sugar, and rum.

This recipe acquires its ginger flavor from three sources: fresh ginger, candied ginger, and ginger cider. If the later is unavailable, you can use ginger ale, apple cider, or milk.

¾ cup good-quality molasses

¾ cup dark brown sugar

½ cup (1 stick) unsalted butter,
   at room temperature

½ cup Ginger Cider (page 123), ginger
   ale, apple cider, or milk

2 tablespoons dark rum

1 tablespoon grated fresh ginger

3 tablespoons finely chopped candied
   ginger

2 eggs, lightly beaten

2 cups all-purpose flour

2 teaspoons baking powder

1 teaspoon baking soda

½ teaspoon ground nutmeg

½ teaspoon ground allspice

Preheat the oven to 350°F. Liberally butter an 8-x-10-inch baking pan and line the bottom with a sheet of parchment paper.

Combine the molasses, brown sugar, butter, ginger beer, rum, grated ginger, and candied ginger in a large, heavy saucepan. Cook over medium heat, stirring with a wooden spoon, until the butter has completely melted and the ingredients are well mixed, about 5 minutes. Remove the pan from the heat and let cool.

Stir the eggs into the molasses mixture. Sift the flour, baking powder, baking soda, nutmeg, and allspice into the molasses mixture. Beat to mix with a wooden spoon.

Transfer the batter to the cake pan and bake the gingerbread until firm, 30 to 40 minutes. An inserted skewer will come out clean when the gingerbread is done. Place the pan on a cake rack to cool. When cooled completely, cut the gingerbread into 2-inch squares and transfer them with a spatula to an airtight tin.

The gingerbread will keep for up to a week.

Makes twenty 2-inch squares.

WEST INDIANS ARE NOTORIOUS for liking sweets. Perhaps this is a legacy from the vast sugarcane plantations that once covered every acre of arable land in the islands. Or the fact that sugar remains one of the main industries of the Caribbean.

In any case, sugary candies and snacks are beloved by West Indians of all nationalities. The following fudge goes by various names on the different islands: *doucelettes au coco* in French, *crema de coco* in Spanish, and coconut fudge in English. If you're in a hurry, you can use canned coconut milk, but be sure it is unsweetened.

2 cups Coconut Milk (page 129)
2¹⁄₂ cups sugar
1 tablespoon butter

1 tablespoon dark rum
1 tablespoon vanilla extract

Combine the coconut milk and sugar in a heavy pan and bring to a boil. Lower the heat slightly and cook the mixture until it reaches the soft ball stage (239°F. on a candy thermometer—see Note).

Remove the pan from the heat and beat in the butter, rum, and vanilla. Beat the fudge with a wooden spoon until it becomes smooth, thick, and creamy like soft ice cream, about 3 minutes. Do not overbeat (the mixture will start to look granular), or the fudge will be dry and crumbly.

Transfer the coconut mixture to a lightly oiled baking sheet and let it cool until firm. Cut the fudge into 2-inch squares and let cool completely. Store the fudge in an airtight container. It will keep for about a week.

Makes 12 pieces.

NOTE: To test the fudge mixture for doneness without a candy thermometer, drop a small spoonful in a bowl of cold water. If it comes together in a soft gummy ball, it has reached the soft ball stage.

T HE SMOOTH MOLDED CUSTARD known as flan was brought to the Caribbean by the Spanish. Today it's popular throughout the West Indies, where it often takes on a distinctly tropical character, thanks to the addition of coconut and local spices.

The following recipe yields individual flans, but you could also make one big one, using an 8-inch cake pan.

For the caramel:
1 cup sugar

For the custard:

1½ cups Coconut Milk (page 129, or canned)	2 teaspoons vanilla extract
1 (14-ounce) ounce can sweetened condensed milk	½ teaspoon ground cinnamon
5 eggs, lightly beaten	¼ teaspoon freshly grated nutmeg
2 tablespoons dark rum	

Prepare the caramel. Combine the sugar and ¼ cup water in a saucepan. Cover the pan and cook over high heat for 2 minutes. Uncover the pan and continue cooking until the sugar mixture caramelizes (turns a deep golden brown), 3 to 4 minutes. Pour a little caramel into each of eight ½-cup ramekins or one 8-inch cake pan and tilt to coat the bottom and sides with caramel. Warning: take care not to drip any caramel on your fingers—it's excruciatingly hot; you may wish to wear gloves to protect your hands. Bring 1 quart of water to a boil. Preheat the oven to 350°F.

Prepare the custard. Combine the coconut milk, sweetened condensed milk, eggs, rum, vanilla, cinnamon, and nutmeg in a mixing bowl and whisk until smooth. Strain this mixture into the ramekins or cake pan. Place the ramekins or pan in a roasting pan with ½ inch boiling water. Place the pan in the oven.

Bake the flans until set, about 30 minutes. When cooked, an inserted toothpick or skewer will come out clean. Transfer to a cake rack and cool to room temperature. Refrigerate the flans for at least 6 hours, preferably overnight.

Just before serving, run the tip of a paring knife around the inside edge of each ramekin or cake pan. Place a dessert plate over each and invert the flan onto the plate. (You may need to give the flans a little shake.) Spoon any caramel that remains in the ramekin over and around the flan.

Serves 8.

DRINKS AND DRINK MIXES

Simple Syrup

SIMPLE SYRUP IS THE STARTING POINT for a host of Caribbean cocktails. Most bartenders in the islands use bottled cane syrup. I prefer this quick and easy homemade version, to which you can add such sun-belt flavorings as lemon or orange zest, vanilla, or cinnamon.

NOTE: The zest is the oil-rich outer rind of a citrus fruit. Wash the fruit thoroughly, then remove the zest in broad, thin strips with a vegetable peeler. Be sure to take only the zest (the outer rind), not the bitter white pith beneath it.

2 cups sugar
2 strips lemon zest
2 strips orange zest

$\frac{1}{2}$ vanilla bean, cut in half
  lengthwise (optional)
1 cinnamon stick, 3 inches long (optional)

Combine the sugar, zests, vanilla, and cinnamon stick with 2 cups water in a heavy saucepan and gradually bring to a boil without stirring. Remove the pan from the heat and let the syrup cool to room temperature. Strain it into a jar or bottle. Store Simple Syrup in the refrigerator; it will keep almost indefinitely.

Makes 2 cups.

VARIATION: Make the syrup using light or dark brown sugar instead of granulated. This type of syrup is excellent for the fruit punches in this book.

This "punch" is actually an infusion of fresh passion fruit and spices in rum. Passion fruit is a round, leathery-skinned, yellow, brown, or purple fruit whose bright orange pulp harbors a myriad of tiny black seeds. The pulp has the tartness of lime juice, the fragrance of jasmine, and a perfumed flavor reminiscent of pineapple. This recipe comes from my friend Jean-Claude Plassais, an avid gardener and owner of the charming Yuana Hotel in St. Barthélemy.

Passion fruit is sold at Hispanic and Asian markets, upscale greengrocers, and an increasing number of supermarkets. In areas with a large Hispanic population, it's sometimes sold by its Spanish name, *maracuja*. When buying passion fruit, look for large spheres that feel heavy in your hand. It's normal for a passion fruit to look creased or partially deflated. In fact, if it's too round, it may not be fully ripe.

8 passion fruits (about 1 cup pulp)

6 to 7 tablespoons brown sugar

1 (1-liter) bottle white rum

1 vanilla bean, cut in half lengthwise

1 cinnamon stick, 3 inches long

Cut the passion fruits in half and scrape the pulp into a 2-cup measuring cup. Add the brown sugar and stir until the sugar is dissolved. Note how much mixture you have. Pour an equal amount of rum out of the bottle. Replace with the passion fruit mixture, vanilla bean, and cinnamon stick. Reseal the bottle.

Place the punch in a cool, dark place and let stand for at least 2 weeks or as much as 2 months. (The longer the punch sits, the more flavorful and mellow it will be.) Store in a cool, dark place; it will keep almost indefinitely.

To serve, pour the punch into glasses filled with ice. Or serve straight up. Yes, you can eat any passion fruit seeds that find their way into the glass. Bite them for a distinctive and pleasurable crunch.

Makes 1 liter.

Tamarind Water and Nectar

The curved brown pod of the tall, tropical tamarind tree turns up at markets throughout the Caribbean. You've probably tasted it—even if you've never heard of it—for tamarind is a key flavoring in such popular table sauces as Worcestershire, Pickapeppa, and A.1.

The tamarind fruit is a long, stiff, curved pod that contains a tart, fruity, slightly sweet orange-brown pulp. The fruit takes its name from the Arabic words *tamr hindi*, literally "Indian date." Actually, tamarind paste tastes more like prunes than dates—prunes mixed with lime juice and a drop of Liquid Smoke.

This distinctive sweet-sour flavor has endeared tamarind to cooks throughout the West Indies. Today you can find tamarind chutney in Trinidad, tamarind candies in Barbados, tamarind barbecue sauce in Jamaica, tamarind nectar in Cuba, and tamarind sodas in Puerto Rico.

Tamarind is beginning to turn up in American restaurants and gourmet shops. You can also find it at Hispanic and West Indian markets and even at progressive supermarkets. When buying tamarind pods, look for fleshy ones that feel heavy when you hold them. When tamarind is ripe, the skin cracks open, revealing the sticky pulp. Avoid smooth pods with intact skin; they're likely to be underripe.

Stringy and riddled with seeds, tamarind is seldom used in its natural state. The first step is to transform the sticky flesh into tamarind water, also known as tamarind puree. This is done by pureeing peeled tamarind pods with boiling water. This isn't difficult, but it is time-consuming. The process is outlined below.

Use tamarind water to add piquancy to curries, chutneys, stews, soups, and sauces. Add it to any dish that could benefit from the tartness of lime, but with a touch of fruity sweetness. To make Tamarind Nectar, combine 1 cup tamarind water with 4 cups cold water, adding sugar to taste.

½ pound tamarind pods (8 to 10 pods)
1½ cups boiling water

Peel the skin off the tamarind pods with a paring knife. Break the pulp into 1-inch pieces and place in the bowl of a blender with 1 cup boiling water. Let the tamarind soften for 5 minutes.

Run the blender in short bursts at low speed for 15 to 20 seconds to obtain a thick brown liquid. Do not overblend, or you'll break up the seeds. Pour the resulting liquid through a strainer, pressing hard with a wooden spoon to extract the juices, scraping the bottom of the strainer with a spatula.

Return the pulp in the strainer to the blender and add ½ cup boiling water. Blend again and pour the mixture though the strainer, pressing well to extract the juices.

Tamarind water will keep for up to 5 days in the refrigerator and can be frozen for several months. I like to freeze it in plastic ice-cube trays so I have convenient portions.

Makes about 1 cup.

NOTE: There are two tamarind convenience products on the market. The first is peeled, destringed tamarind pulp, which is sold in plastic packages at Asian and Hispanic markets. The second is frozen tamarind puree, available at Hispanic markets.

Tamarind Syrup

TAMARIND SYRUP IS THE BASE of a refreshing soda enjoyed throughout the Spanish Caribbean. Place an inch or so of the syrup in the bottom of a tall glass and fill the glass with club soda. Stir well.

1 cup sugar
1 cup tamarind water

Combine the sugar and ½ cup of water in a heavy saucepan and bring to a rolling boil. Add the tamarind water and simmer until the mixture is thick and syrupy, 5 to 10 minutes. Using a shallow ladle, skim off any foam that rises to the surface as the syrup cooks.

Transfer the syrup to sterile jars filled to within ⅛ inch of the top (see page 13). Tightly screw on the lid. Let the syrup cool to room temperature, then refrigerate. Tamarind syrup will keep for several weeks in the refrigerator.

Makes 1½ cups.

Pineapple Punch

A HANDSOME DISPLAY OF FRUIT PUNCHES is the pride of any self-respecting bar or restaurant in the French West Indies. The prize for the best collection may well go to the Bar at the Deux Mamelles Zoo in Guadaloupe, where more than seventy different punches are displayed.

The theory behind these inviting punches is simple enough: rum is macerated for several weeks or even months with ripe fruit and simple syrup. The vessel of choice is a large, widemouthed glass jar. Fruit punch makes an attractive centerpiece for a buffet table, not to mention an extraordinary present.

Here's a basic recipe using pineapple, but you can use any ripe tropical fruit, including banana, guava, mango, papaya, carambola, soursop, lychee, or Barbados cherry. The fruit can be diced or sliced or, for a more dramatic presentation, left whole.

1 very ripe pineapple
4 to 5 cups white rum, or as needed
About 1 cup Simple Syrup made with
  brown sugar (page 116)

1 cinnamon stick, 3 inches long
1 vanilla bean, cut in half lengthwise

Remove the leaves from the pineapple. A simple way to do this is to grab the fruit in one hand, the leaves in the other, and twist in opposite directions. Thoroughly wash the pineapple, scrubbing the skin with a brush, and cut it lengthwise in quarters, working over a bowl to catch any juices.

Place the pineapple quarters in a large, widemouthed jar. Add half the rum, followed by the syrup, cinnamon stick, and vanilla bean. Add any reserved pineapple juices and enough rum to fill the jar to the top.

Tightly cover the jar and let the fruit macerate in a cool, dark spot for 4 to 8 weeks or even longer. (The longer the maceration, the smoother the punch will be.)

Just before serving, gently stir the punch with a wooden spoon. (The sugar tends to sink to the bottom of the jar.) Taste the punch for sweetness, adding syrup if desired.

The punch can be served over ice or straight up. As the level of the punch goes down, you can add fresh rum and syrup.

Makes about 1 quart.

NOTE: For the best results, use a very ripe, very sweet pineapple. Look for two signs of sweetness when buying the fruit. The first is the color: a gold or yellow rind indicates an advanced stage of ripeness. The second is the aroma: the base of a ripe pineapple will smell distinctly fruity. The "super-sweet" gold pineapple marketed by Dole works well.

Falernum

FALERNUM BELONGS to a venerable family of syrupy rum punches that enjoyed great vogue in the Caribbean in the eighteenth century. It seems to have been named for a famous wine from the Italian province of Campania, much beloved by the ancient Romans. The almond extract gives falernum a flavor unique among Caribbean rum drinks.

During the colonial period, falernum was enjoyed as a beverage in its own right. It was used as a flavoring for cocktails in North America through the early part of this century. Even today, falernum with rum and coconut water remains a popular plantation drink in Barbados. (The proportions are roughly 1 tablespoon falernum, 3 tablespoons rum, and 1 cup coconut water.)

I say it's time to rediscover a beverage that makes not only a welcome addition to fruit punches and rum drinks but a pleasurable after-dinner drink served over ice.

1¼ cups sugar

1 cup fresh lime juice

1 cup white rum

½ teaspoon almond extract

Combine the sugar and 1 cup of water in a large, heavy saucepan and bring to a boil, stirring well. When the sugar is completely dissolved, remove the pan from the heat and let cool.

Add the lime juice, rum, and almond extract and stir until mixed. Transfer the Falernum to bottles and store in a cool, dark place until serving. Tradition calls for the Falernum to be aged 6 months, but it will be palatable after just a few days. Falernum will keep almost indefinitely.

Makes 2½ cups.

Nᴇᴡ ᴇɴɢʟᴀɴᴅ ᴍᴇᴇᴛs ᴛʜᴇ ᴄᴀʀɪʙʙᴇᴀɴ in this spicy cousin of ginger ale. Ginger beer is enjoyed throughout the West Indies, especially in Trinidad and Jamaica, where every family has a treasured recipe handed down through generations. You may be surprised to learn that not all ginger beer is carbonated. Many families enjoy fresh, nonfermented ginger beer, which is more like a Ginger Cider.

A great many misconceptions surround ginger, not the least of which is that it's a root. Actually, it's a rhizome (an underground stem) that has both leaves and roots. The stems and leaves resemble those of bamboo; the flowers are incredibly fragrant.

When buying fresh ginger, look for firm springy "hands" (as clusters of ginger are called in the trade) that feel heavy when you hold them. Avoid ginger that looks shriveled or wilted. The younger the ginger, the more tender and mild flavored it will be. Older ginger tends to be fibrous and hot.

A quick, easy way to give this cider zing is to put it in a siphon bottle and spritz it.

4 ounces fresh ginger	1 cup raw (turbinado) sugar, or to taste
2 strips lime zest	1 quart boiling water
2 whole cloves	3 tablespoons fresh lime juice

Wash the ginger and coarsely grate or puree in a food processor. Transfer the ginger to a large glass jar or earthenware crock. Stick the cloves in the lime zest and add the sugar, boiling water, and lime juice and stir until the sugar is dissolved. Loosely cover the jar with a clean kitchen towel and let stand in a cool, dark place for 24 hours.

Strain the Ginger Cider into clean glass bottles and refrigerate until serving. The Ginger Cider will keep for several weeks in the refrigerator.

Makes 1 quart.

Guava Nectar

ONE OF EASIEST AND MOST PLEASURABLE ways to enjoy guava is in nectar form. Until I moved to Miami, I had only experienced canned juice. Fresh guava nectar came as a revelation.

Guava nectar makes an exotic, refreshing beverage in its own right and is an essential ingredient in many Caribbean cocktails, including Planter's Punch (see page 130).

1 pound ripe guavas
¼ to ½ cup sugar, or to taste
2 tablespoons fresh lime juice

Wash the guavas and trim off any blemishes or hard parts. Thinly slice the fruit and place it in a large saucepan with 3 cups water and ¼ cup sugar. Bring the guavas to a boil.

Reduce the heat and simmer the guavas until very soft, about 20 minutes. Add more water as necessary to keep the guavas submerged. Let the mixture cool slightly. Transfer it to a blender and puree.

Pour the mixture through a strainer into a large jar or pitcher, pressing with a rubber spatula or the back of a wooden spoon to extract as much liquid as possible. Let the nectar cool completely.

Stir in the lime juice and taste for sweetness, adding sugar as desired. Refrigerate the guava nectar until serving. It will keep for about a week. Stir the guava nectar just before serving.

Makes 1 quart.

Here's a delectable punch that comes in a distinctive container: a hollowed coconut. Tips on buying coconuts are found on page 110. For a more perfumed punch you can add a little more Simple Syrup or a small piece of vanilla bean.

1 large ripe (hard) coconut

2 cups white rum, or as needed

2 to 3 tablespoons Simple Syrup
   (optional, page 116)

1 piece of vanilla bean, 1 inch
   long (optional)

Punch out two of the eyes of the coconut using a screwdriver and hammer. Invert the coconut over a glass and let the coconut water drain out.

Using a small funnel, fill the coconut to the top with rum. For a sweeter punch, add the syrup or vanilla bean. Cut tiny plugs out of a wine cork and use them to stop the holes in the coconut. Light a candle and drip wax over the corks to form hermetic seals.

Let the punch "ripen" in the coconut for 2 weeks to 2 months. (The longer it sits, the richer the flavor.) Store in a cool, dark place; it will keep almost indefinitely.

To serve, scrape the wax off with a knife and unplug the holes. Drain the rum into a pitcher or glasses. Serve it straight up or over ice. Alternatively, you could chill the whole coconut in the refrigerator and insert a slender straw for sipping.

Makes about 2 cups.

NOTE: After a month of aging, the vessel becomes as tasty as the liquid inside. Crack the coconut open, following instructions on page 104, and serve the rum-scented flesh.

'Ti Punch

'TI PUNCH (short for *petit* punch, "little punch") is the French West Indian version of a Manhattan. You find it at beach bars in Martinique, four-star hotels in St. Martin, and everywhere in between.

It certainly lives up to the name "little," consisting of little more than straight rum jazzed up with a splash of syrup and lime juice. To be strictly authentic, you would use a French rum, such as St. James from Martinique or Père Labat from Marie Galante, but other rums will work.

OPPOSITE, FROM LEFT TO RIGHT *Passion Fruit Punch (page 117), Guava Nectar (page 124), Simple Syrup (page 116), Falernum (page 122), 'Ti Punch, Coconut Punch (page 125), and Pineapple Punch (page 120)*

1 jigger (1½ ounces or 3 tablespoons) light or dark rum

1 to 2 teaspoons Simple Syrup, or to taste (page 116)

A wedge of fresh lime

Combine the rum and syrup in a stemmed glass. Ice is optional—add a couple of cubes if you like it. Squeeze a few drops of lime juice into the drink and place the wedge on the rim of the glass. Serve at once, with a swizzle stick for stirring.

Serves 1 and can be multiplied as desired.

Vanilla Rum

MOST PEOPLE USE VANILLA as a flavoring for cookies, cakes, and ice cream. Not Patrick Gateau. The chef of the stunning Carl Gustaf Hotel overlooking Gustavia Harbor in St. Barts stews lobster with vanilla beans, adds the tiny black seeds to a sauce for salmon, and steeps the fragrant black pods in rum. The latter produces an intriguing beverage that's delightful sipped by itself (I like to serve it over ice) or added to your favorite Caribbean rum drink. You can even use it as a flavoring—a sort of homemade vanilla extract.

Native to the rain forests of southern Mexico and Central America, vanilla is grown throughout the Caribbean, from St. Lucia to Guadaloupe. Vanilla beans are generally sold by the piece in glass tubes or bottles. When buying them, seek out fat, pliable pods that feel heavy in your hand. Avoid dried out or brittle beans. To get the maximum flavor from a vanilla bean, cut it in half lengthwise with a sharp knife. The best rum for this recipe is an aged dark rum, like Barbancourt from Haiti.

2 vanilla beans, cut in half lengthwise
1 bottle dark rum

¼ to ½ cup Simple Syrup
(optional, page 116)

Cut the vanilla beans in half lengthwise and add them to the rum. If a sweet rum is desired, pour off ¼ to ½ cup rum and add the Simple Syrup. Let the vanilla beans steep for at least 1 month before serving. The flavor will continue to improve with age.

Makes 1 bottle.

Tᴀɪꜱ ʀɪᴄʜ, ᴍɪʟᴋʏ ʟɪꝗᴜɪᴅ serves as the heavy cream of the tropics. In the days before refrigeration, it was used like a dairy product and it remains an important ingredient in the cooking of Trinidad, Jamaica, and Guadaloupe.

The first thing you need to know about coconut milk is what it isn't. Coconut milk is not the clearish liquid inside the coconut. That's coconut water. (Some cooks use coconut water in the preparation of coconut milk.) Coconut milk is made by blending freshly grated coconut with boiling water. The term "milk" is appropriate, for the resulting mixture behaves like a dairy product.

Coconut milk probably came to the Caribbean with indentured workers from India, brought to work the vast sugarcane plantations in the early nineteenth century after the abolition of slavery. Unlike milk and cream, which spoil quickly in the tropical heat, coconut milk can be stored in the coconut (a nonperishable item if ever there was one) until virtually the moment you need it. It only takes a few minutes to make.

ı ripe (hard) coconut
2 cups boiling water

Pierce the eyes of the coconut with a screwdriver and drain the coconut water through a strainer into a bowl or measuring cup. Open and shell the coconut, removing the brown skin as described on page 104. Break the coconut into 1-inch pieces and grate.

Combine the grated coconut, coconut water, and boiling water in a blender and blend for 3 minutes. Work in several batches if necessary. You don't want to fill the blender too full. (Be sure the cover is on tightly. You may wish to cover the top of the blender with a dish cloth for added protection.) Let the mixture stand for 10 to 15 minutes. Pour the mixture through a fine mesh strainer or a strainer lined with several layers of cheesecloth. Twist the cheesecloth tightly to extract as much milk as possible.

Store coconut milk in the refrigerator, where it will keep for 3 to 4 days. It can also be frozen.

Makes about 2 cups.

The "Cooking in Paradise" Planter's Punch

PLANTER'S PUNCH IS A TRADITIONAL drink of welcome throughout the Caribbean. The basic formula runs equal parts orange, pineapple, and guava nectar and rum. But everyone has strong opinions about particular flavorings and garnishes. Here's the one we serve at my cooking school, Cooking in Paradise, in St. Barthélemy.

1 cup dark rum	½ teaspoon angostura bitters
1 cup fresh orange juice	4 cinnamon sticks, 3 inches long
1 cup pineapple juice (preferably fresh)	4 fresh pineapple rings
2 tablespoons lime juice	4 orange slices
1 cup Guava Nectar (page 124)	4 maraschino cherries
3 tablespoons Simple Syrup, or	Freshly grated nutmeg to taste
to taste (page 116)	Ice

Combine the rum, orange, pineapple, and lime juices, guava nectar, syrup, and bitters in a pitcher and stir with a wooden spoon until the sugar is dissolved.

Fill 4 bar glasses with 3 or 4 ice cubes each and fill with punch. Garnish each glass with a cinnamon stick, pineapple ring, orange slice, and maraschino cherry. Grate a little nutmeg over each punch and serve at once.

Serves 4.

THE SPICY LIQUEUR KNOWN AS SHRUB is a traditional holiday drink in St. Martin. Made in early December, it is uncorked on Christmas Eve. Tradition calls for the rum and flavorings to be infused in a glass jar in the sun for a month. I've redesigned the recipe so that you can make it in a single morning.

Shrub is traditionally sipped after the meal, as you would a cordial or liqueur. It can also be mixed with an equal volume of rum, stirred with ice, and served as an apéritif.

2 oranges

2 tangerines

2 lemons

2 cinnamon sticks, 3 inches long

20 whole cloves

20 allspice berries

1 vanilla bean, split in half

3 cups sugar

8 cups white rum

Wash the fruits. Using a vegetable peeler, remove the zest (oil-rich outer rind) in strips, avoiding the bitter white pith. Combine the citrus zest, cinnamon sticks, cloves, allspice, vanilla bean, 2 cups sugar, and 2 cups water in a saucepan. Bring to a gentle boil, reduce the heat to the lowest possible setting, and let the ingredients infuse for 30 minutes. Strain the syrup into a large mixing bowl.

Combine the remaining 1 cup sugar and ½ cup water in a large, deep, heavy saucepan. Cover the pan and bring the mixture to a boil. Uncover the pan and cook the mixture over high heat until it caramelizes (turns golden brown), about 5 minutes. Remove the pan from the heat and let cool for 5 minutes.

Add 1 cup rum to the caramel. Be careful: the mixture may spatter. When the spattering has subsided, return the pan to low heat and cook the mixture, stirring with a wooden spoon, until the caramel has dissolved in the rum.

Add the caramel mixture and remaining rum to the citrus-flavored syrup. Whisk to mix. With the aid of a funnel, pour the mixture into clean bottles. Seal with corks.

The shrub is ready to drink now, but it will be even better if you leave it for a week or so to allow the flavors to blend. Store in a cool, dark place.

Makes about 2 quarts.

Acknowledgments

THE CARIBBEAN PANTRY COOKBOOK was a joy to write, but it wasn't all rum drinks and coconut cakes. The author would like to thank the many people who worked hard to make this book happen:

My thanks to Artisan publisher, Leslie Stoker, who encouraged me to write this book, Ann ffolliott, who polished it with her skillful editing, and Martin Jacobs, who brought the recipes alive with his lovely photographs. I'd also like to thank Linda Johnson, William Smith, Donna Sebro, Marianne Smith, Joe Cirincione, Carole Berglie, Arlene Lee, Beth Wareham, Jim Wageman, Hope Koturo, Marcia Pomerantz, and Jennifer Hong. A big thanks, too, to Peter Workman, Andrea Bass Glickson, and the whole crew at Workman.

Another big thanks to Sharon Morrisson, recipe tester extraordinaire and cooking friend from Barbados. Once again, Elida Proenza was our Cuban connection as well as being a great cook and a great friend.

I would also like to thank Horace Hord and Gisela Yacosa of American Airlines; Michael De Peaza, Nancy Pierre, and Tony Poyer of the Trinidad Tourism Development Bureau; Patricia Hannan and Jackie Murray of the Jamaica Tourist Board; Traci La Rosa and Mark

Walsh of Peter Martin Associates, Inc; Myron Clement and Joe Petrocik of the Clement-Petrocik Co.; Winston Stoner of Busha Browne's Company, Ltd.; the Barbados Board of Tourism; the Curaçao Tourist Development Bureau; the French West Indies Tourist Board; and Marc and Kiki Ellenby of LNB Groves in Homestead, Florida.

My thanks also to some of our friends from St. Barts, including Eric Troncani and Patrick Gateau of the Carl Gustaf Hotel; Michel Ledee of the Marigot Bay Club; Madeleine and Jean-Claude Plassais of the Hotel Yuana, and all my students at The Cooking in Paradise Cooking School.

Finally, a big thanks to my family—Betsy, Jake, Marc (who is almost family), and especially Barbara, my wife and Caribbean playmate, who survived yet another book and session of recipe testing.

Conversion Chart

Ingredients and Equipment Glossary

British English and American English are not always the same, particularly in the kitchen. The following ingredients and equipment used in this book are pretty much the same on both sides of the Atlantic, but have different names:

AMERICAN	BRITISH
bell pepper	sweet pepper (capsicum)
broiler/to broil	grill/to grill
celery stalk	celery stick
chili pepper	chilli
confectioners' sugar	icing sugar
cornstarch	cornflour
fava bean	broad bean
heavy cream (37.6% fat)	double cream (35-40% fat)
molasses	treacle
peanut	groundnut
scallion	spring onion
seeds	pips
seeded	stoned
skillet	frying pan
tuna	tunny
vanilla bean	vanilla pod

Butter

Some confusion may arise over the measuring of butter and other hard fats. In the United States, butter is generally sold in a one-pound package, which contains four equal "sticks." The wrapper on each stick is marked to show tablespoons, so the cook can cut the stick according to the quantity required. The equivalent weights are:

1 stick = 115 g/4 oz
1 T = 15 g/ ½ oz

Eggs

Unless otherwise noted, all recipes in this book use American large-size eggs, which are equivalent to British standard-size eggs.

Flour

American all-purpose flour is milled from a mixture of hard and soft wheats, whereas British plain flour is made mainly from soft wheat. To achieve a near equivalent to American all-purpose flour, use half British plain flour and half strong bread flour.

Gelatin

Quantities of unflavored powdered gelatin are usually given in envelopes, each of which contains 7 g/¼ oz (about 1 tablespoon).

Sugar

In the recipes in this book, if sugar is called for it is assumed to be granulated, unless otherwise specified. American granulated sugar is finer than British granulated, closer to caster sugar.

Oven Temperature Equivalents

OVEN	°F.	°C.	GAS MARK
very cool	250–275	130–140	½–1
cool	300	150	2
warm	325	170	3
moderate	350	180	4
moderately hot	375	190	5
	400	200	6
hot	425	220	7
very hot	450	230	8
	475	250	9
	500	260	10

Volume Equivalents

These are not exact equivalents for the American cups and spoons, but have been rounded up or down slightly to make measuring easier.

AMERICAN	METRIC	IMPERIAL
1¼ t	1.25 ml	
½ t	2.5 ml	
1 t	5 ml	
½ T (1½ t)	7.5 ml	
1 T (3 t)	15 ml	
¼ cup (4 T)	60 ml	2 fl. oz
⅓ cup (5 T)	75 ml	2½ fl oz
½ cup (8 T)	125 ml	4 fl oz
⅔ cup (10 T)	150 ml	5 fl oz (¼ pint)
¾ cup (12 T)	175 ml	6 fl oz
1 cup (16 T)	250 ml	8 fl oz
1¼ cups	300 ml	10 fl oz
1½ cups	350 ml	12 fl oz
1 pint (2 cups)	500 ml	16 fl oz
1 quart (4 cups)	1 litre	1¾ pints

Weight Equivalents

The metric weights given in this chart are not exact equivalents, but have been rounded up or down slightly to make measuring easier.

IMPERIAL	METRIC
¼ oz	7 g
½ oz	15 g
1 oz	30 g
2 oz	60 g
3 oz	90 g
4 oz	115 g
5 oz	150 g
6 oz	175 g
7 oz	200 g
8 oz (½ lb)	225 g
9 oz	250 g
10 oz	300 g
11 oz	325 g
12 oz	350 g
13 oz	375 g
14 oz	400 g
15 oz	425 g
16 oz (1 lb)	450 g
1 lb 2 oz	500 g
1½ lb	750 g
2 lb	900 g
2¼ lb	1 kg
3 lb	1.4 kg
4 lb	1.8 kg
4½ lb	2 kg

Mail-Order Sources

Many Caribbean ingredients are available in supermarkets and in West Indian markets. If you can't locate ingredients, here are some places that provide mail-order service:

Adriana's Caravan
409 Vanderbilt Street
Brooklyn, NY 11218
(800) 316-0820
(718) 436-8565

Mail-order only; Catalogue available

Assouline & Ting
314 Brown Street
Philadelphia, PA 19123
(215) 627-3000

Catalogue available

Cardullo's Gourmet Shop
6 Brattle Street
Cambridge, MA 02138
(617) 491-8888

Caribbean Food Products, Inc.
1936 North Second Avenue
Jacksonville Beach, FL 32250
(904) 246-0149
Fax (904) 246-7273

Coyote Cafe General Store
132 West Water Street
Santa Fe, NM 87501
(505) 982-2454

Catalogue available

DeKalb's World Farmers Market
3000 E. Ponce De Leon
Decatur, GA 30034
(404) 377-6401

Dean and DeLuca
560 Broadway
New York, NY 10012
(212) 431-1691

Catalogue available

Freida's By Mail
P.O. Box 58488
Los Angeles, CA 90058
(800) 241-1771
(714) 826-6100

Mail-order only; Catalogue available

Jamaica Groceries & Spices
9587 S.W. 160th Street
Miami, FL 33157
(305) 252-1197

Kingston-Miami Trading Co.
280 N.E. Second St.
Miami, FL 33132
(305) 372-9547
or
1500 N.W. 22nd Street
Miami, FL 33142
(305) 324-0231

Catalogue available

Melissa's by Mail
P. O. Box 21127
Los Angeles, CA 90021
(800)588-0151

Catalogue available

Not Just Coffee
4229 Main Street
Manayunk, PA 19127
(215)482-8582

Catalogue available

Ocho-Rios Miami Trading Co.
2051 N.W. 15th Ave.
Miami, FL 33142
(305) 326-1734

Catalogue available

Penzey's Ltd. Spice House
P. O. Box 1448
Waukesha, WI 53187
(414)574-0277

Catalogue available

Royal Distributors
1275 Bennett Drive, Suite 140
Longwood, FL 32750
(407) 332-0008

Bibliography

Barrow, Errol W. and Kendal A. Lee. *Privilege: Cooking in the Caribbean*. Hong Kong: Macmillan Publishers Ltd, 1988.

Benjamin, Floella. *Floella Benjamin's Caribbean Cookery*. London: Century Hutchinson Ltd., 1986.

Browne, Busha. *Busha Browne's Indispensable Compendium of Traditional Jamaican Cookery*. Jamaica: The Mill Press Ltd., 1993.

Creen, Linette. *A Taste of Cuba*. New York: Penguin Group, 1991.

DeWitt, Dave and Mary Jane Wilan. *Callaloo, Calypso, & Carnival*. Freedom, California: The Crossing Press, 1993.

Donaldson, Enid. *The Real Taste of Jamaica*. Jamaica: Ian Randle Publishers Limited, 1993.

Elbert, Virginie F. and George A. Elbert. *Down-Island Caribbean Cookery*. New York: Simon & Schuster, 1991.

Fenzi, Jewell. *This the Way We Cook!* (Asina Nos Ta Cushina). Netherlands: Thayer-Sargent, 1971.

Harris, Dunstan A. *Island Barbecue: Spirited Recipes from the Caribbean*. San Francisco: Chronicle Books, 1995.

Harris, Jessica. *Sky Juice and Flying Fish*. New York: Fireside, 1991.

Hamilton, Jill. *Taste of Barbados*. N.p.: Letchworth Press, Ltd., n.d.

Huyke, Giovanna. *La Cocina Puertorriqueña De Hoy*. Puerto Rico: Esmaco Printers Corp., 1992.

Idone, Christopher. *Cooking Caribe*. New York: Potter, 1992.

Mackie, Christine. *Life and Food in the Caribbean*. New York: New Amsterdam, 1991.

Mahabir, Kumar. *Caribbean East Indian Recipes*. Trinidad: Chakra Publishing House, 1992.

Mathura, Ingrid. *Come, Let Us Cook In The Caribbean*. Canada: Gateway Publishing Co. Ltd., 1986.

Naparima Girls' High School. *Diamond Jubilee Recipe Book*. Trinidad, 1988.

Negre, Dr. Andre. *La Cuisine Antillaise*. Tahiti: Les Editions du Pacifique, 1984.

Ortiz, Elizabeth Lambert. *The Complete Book of Caribbean Cooking*. New York: Ballantine Books, 1986.

Ortiz, Yvonne. *A Taste of Puerto Rico*. New York: The Penguin Group, 1994.

Pringle, John Kenneth McKenzie. *A Collection of 19th Century Jamaican Cookery and Herbal Recipes*. Jamaica: The Mill Press, 1990.

Renault, Jean-Michael. *Le Rhum*. Saint Barthélemy: Les Editions du Pelican, 1988.

Ribere, Roselyne. *La Bonne Cuisine Des Antilles*. Paris: Editions Solar, 1992.

Roy-Camille, Christiane and Annick Marie. *Les Meilleures Recettes De La Cuisine Antillaise*. Belgium: Editions Gamma, 1986.

Sisterhood Board of Mikve Israel-Emanuel. *Recipes From the Jewish Kitchens of Curaçao*. Curaçao: Drukkerij Scherpenheuvel N.V., 1990.

Springer, Rita G. *Caribbean Cookbook*. London: Evans Brothers Ltd., 1979.

Valldejuli, Carmen Aboy. *Puerto Rican Cookery*. Louisiana: Pelican Publishing Co. Inc., 1980.

Index

Page numbers in italic refer to illustrations

SERIES DESIGN/ART DIRECTION: JIM WAGEMAN
DESIGNED BY ARLENE LEE/KAZ AKIYAMA, MIGHTY DIMENSION, INC.
JACKET DESIGNED BY JENNIFER S. HONG

TYPEFACES IN THIS BOOK ARE MONOTYPE DANTE, DESIGNED
BY GIOVANNI MARDERSTEIG; HONDURAS, DESIGNED BY PAUL HICKSON;
AND FRANKLIN GOTHIC, DESIGNED BY MORRIS BENTON

PRINTED AND BOUND BY
ARNOLDO MONDADORI EDITORE S.P.A.
VERONA, ITALY